The Librarian's
NITTY-GRITTY GUIDE TO
CONTENT MARKETING

LAURA SOLOMON

ala
editions

An imprint of the American Library Association
CHICAGO 2016

Laura Solomon is the library services manager for the Ohio Public Library Information Network and the former web applications manager for the Cleveland Public Library. She has been doing web development and design for over fifteen years, in both public libraries and as an independent consultant. She is a 2010 *Library Journal* Mover & Shaker. She has written two books about social media (published by ALA), specifically for libraries. In 2009 she was recognized by the Ohio Library Council for her role in saving more than $147 million of public library funding by using social media. As a former children's librarian, she enjoys bringing the "fun of technology" to audiences and in giving libraries the tools they need to better serve the virtual customer.

Extensive effort has gone into ensuring the reliability of the information in this book; however, the publisher makes no warranty, express or implied, with respect to the material contained herein.

ISBNs
978-0-8389-1432-8 (paper)
978-0-8389-1435-9 (PDF)
978-0-8389-1436-6 (ePub)
978-0-8389-1437-3 (Kindle)

Library of Congress Cataloging-in-Publication Data

Names: Solomon, Laura, 1967- author.
Title: The librarian's nitty-gritty guide to content marketing / Laura Solomon.
Other titles: Content marketing
Description: Chicago : ALA Editions, An imprint of the American Library Association, 2016. | Includes bibliographical references and index.
Identifiers: LCCN 2015046381| ISBN 9780838914328 (print : alk. paper) | ISBN 9780838914359 (pdf) | ISBN 9780838914366 (epub) | ISBN 9780838914373 (kindle)
Subjects: LCSH: Libraries—Marketing. | Relationship marketing. | Libraries—Customer services. | Internet marketing. | Organizational effectiveness.
Classification: LCC Z716.3 .S645 2016 | DDC 021.7—dc23 LC record available at http://lccn.loc.gov/2015046381

Cover design by Alejandra Diaz. Imagery © Shutterstock, Inc.
Text design and composition by Kirstin McDougall in the Caecilia LT Std and Melbourne typefaces.

♾ This paper meets the requirements of ANSI/NISO Z39.48–1992 (Permanence of Paper).

Printed in the United States of America

20 19 18 17 16   5 4 3 2 1

The Librarian's
NITTY-GRITTY GUIDE TO
CONTENT
MARKETING

ALA Editions purchases fund advocacy, awareness, and accreditation programs for library professionals worldwide.

Contents

Get Over Yourself

"Success flows to organizations that inform,
not organizations that promote."
—Jay Baer, *Youtility*

Several years ago I was asked to come up with a presentation about how to improve the online presence of a library. The organization wanted me to talk to a group of new library directors, not only about websites, but also about social media work. At first, a lot of disparate things tumbled through my mind: usability, accessibility, metrics, engagement, and all sorts of other buzzwords. Any one of these things would easily rate an hour of discussion, but I needed to narrow it down to something that was meaningful and could be conveyed in a short amount of time. What were the things that really mattered? With only an hour, what needed to be the big takeaway?

CHAPTER 1

I spent some time considering the most common online mistakes I've seen by libraries. I looked at a lot of library websites and social media accounts. While the number of issues was many, I kept coming back to the idea of finding what all or most of the issues actually had in common. Why did I keep seeing the same mistakes, over and over? Why were so many problems related to how libraries attempt to promote themselves? After a lot of thought, I realized that there was really just one underlying concept that makes anything actually effective online. Without doing this one thing, it won't matter what kind of fancy-schmancy website a library has or how many different things it posts to social media channels.

They needed to get over themselves.

An effective online presence really comes down to not putting one's ego first. That could be the collective ego of the library as an institution, the ego of the director, the ego of the board of trustees, or the ego of that territorial staff member who controls the library's online content with an iron fist. It's easy to tell, online, when a library is operating from ego or not. Think about the following scenarios and whom they actually aim to please:

+ Social media accounts that only post program and event announcements
+ Event announcements that are only about those at the library, not the community
+ A library blog that gets virtually no engagement (and staff keep writing it, anyway)
+ Social media accounts that sit, inactive, for days, weeks or even months
+ Blog posts full of paragraphs of text and little else
+ Maintaining online content, such as links lists or pathfinders, that metrics show gets few (if any) visits
+ A website full of pages that haven't been updated in months or years

+ Online program announcements that tell readers how exciting the program will be, but provide no description of actual benefits to be gained by attending

I've seen each of these scenarios multiple times (and I'm betting you have, also), and the one thing they all have in common is that the library prioritized the needs of itself over those of its users. Many libraries only do what's easy or comfortable for them online. Sometimes there are logistical reasons for this, but mostly there aren't, and good planning should have prevented the vast majority of them, anyway.

As soon as any person or entity's ego overrides the needs of the user, the library, as a whole, loses. People will only care about your library's content if it has some value for them. Content that is completely self-serving or self-promotional is an active turnoff. When libraries, like so many other organizations, are struggling to get their online content seen, it's hardly a good idea to continue with strategies that are known to turn people away.

I encourage you to take a long, hard look at what your library does online. Are you really doing it for the online patron, or to please someone/something internally? A library is only effective online when it realizes that the people reading the content matter more than the people creating it.

While the rest of this book is about content marketing and how to do it better, it's essential that you first make a cognitive leap. Stop thinking that everything your library does online is purely about promoting itself, and at least begin to understand that you need to have the benefit for the reader in mind first and foremost. Jay Bauer, a digital marketing expert and author, refers to this idea as "Youtility"[1]:

> Youtility is marketing upside down. Instead of marketing that's needed by companies, Youtility is marketing that's wanted by

customers. Youtility is massively useful information, provided for free, that creates long-term trust and kinship between your company and your customers.[2]

For many libraries, this idea represents a huge shift in the online marketing paradigm. Social media, in particular, has long represented little beyond a promotional opportunity for libraries, with little understanding that social media was never designed for marketing. (For more about this, see my previous book, *The Librarian's Nitty-Gritty Guide to Social Media*.) Libraries represent an abundance of information, but few if any ever capitalize on that asset to make themselves invaluable, or a Youtility, to their communities.

The fact that libraries have not generally taken advantage of this kind of strategy is somewhat bewildering, considering that they are probably one of the organizations least likely to ever run out of content. This situation is probably due to the perspective that most libraries have about marketing in general: still very much entrenched in the broadcast model of sending promotional messages out to the masses (especially only about events), rather than considering how those messages might actually be useful to the masses.

Think about it this way: If your library was considering a renovation to its physical space, would it do it without considering the needs of patrons? Sure, the library's staff would be asked for opinions, but would a library seriously undertake a major overhaul without consulting any end users? Unlikely. Most libraries do surveys, either formally or informally. Some libraries even put out furniture and carpet samples for comparison, and ask patrons for their votes. Some have public meetings. The methods vary, but the goal is the same: The library wants the space to be as useful and appealing as possible for its patrons.

Today, most libraries are very clear that they primarily exist to serve their communities. Yet, these same libraries often fail to apply this logic to what they post online. We inherently understand that we need to make our physical spaces useful and appealing to the people who see and use them. Why don't we do this with the content our libraries produce for people online?

The true core of marketing has never been about promotion. Marketing supports the goals of a business or organization, and promotion is but one way to do that. Philip Kotler and Nancy Lee, marketing professors and authors, write:

> Marketing's central concern is producing outcomes that the target market values. In the private sector, marketing's mantra is customer value and satisfaction. In the public sector, marketing's mantra is citizen value and satisfaction.[3]

Note the end goal for each target audience in the above quote is not to promote anything; it's not even to sell more goods or services. It's to make the recipients happy. Consider how different that is from how most libraries think of marketing goals. Getting more patrons into a program serves the library, not the patrons. Same for increasing circulation statistics or door counts. Those goals are actually byproducts of the real goal: to increase the library's value to its patrons.

Content marketing, done well, can help a library to meet this goal (I'll discuss this more in chapter 3). More importantly, content marketing can help *patrons*. This is the cognitive leap you'll need to make: understanding that being useful and relevant is much more important than the need to send the message.

Thinking about the Payoff

I was once asked what advice I would give someone just starting out in public speaking. Would joining Toastmasters help? Speaking in front of a mirror? I'm still not sure what the best advice would have been, but I explained how I came to be comfortable with presenting. In my first career, I was an environmental/outdoor education teacher. My job was to keep inner city kids interested in things like the life cycles of frogs and the dietary habits of turkey vultures,[+] possibly while it was cold, pouring rain, and the kids had no expensive Gortex raincoats. One learned very fast to make these topics interesting, or 1) the final evaluations from the visiting parents and teachers would rip one to shreds and 2) the kids would probably beat them to it out of sheer boredom.[++]

However, "interesting" is a tricky word and can mean something different from one person to the next. I discovered quickly that I needed to replace that word with the word "relevant." It was my job to make my classes relevant to those kids, to the point where they not only weren't bored, but could make some kind of personal connection to the information I was providing. Without that personal connection, that information would almost assuredly go in one ear and out the other. In other words, it was my professional responsibility to give them a reason to care.

So let's bring this around to libraries. Of course, we're concerned about our own relevancy in this increasingly digital era. But I think we get very focused on this aspect and can lose sight of the fact that we, too, have a professional responsibility to give people a reason to care. True, many libraries are seeing large increases in usage. The sagging economy suddenly propelled us to relevancy in the eyes of people who were/are trimming budgets. However, I want to bring this down to a more micro-level approach. Think about individual services you provide in your library and how they are marketed.

[+] Turkey vultures are actually very cool birds. Most predators won't mess with them because one of their primary methods of defense is voluntary regurgitation; yes, that's right—they throw up on their enemies. And, remember what turkey vultures eat. Carrion. Fun times. (And of immense interest to kids, of course.)

[++] I actually LOVED this job.

Remember, my job wasn't to make every kid that came through our program want to join Greenpeace, the Sierra Club, or to immediately go out and save the world; it was to connect them personally to the environment as a whole through connections to smaller, digestible parts. Libraries could be doing the same thing. For every event your library wants to promote, ask the question, "What does this mean to me, Library?" In this instance, "me" is the average patron who has way too many demands on her time, is desperately seeking a new job, trying to sell his house, finishing a degree . . . you get the idea. What will the average "I don't have time" person gain from this? Will this story time expose my child to literacy activities that will help him in school? Will my cover letters stand out? Could my house sell faster or for more money?

At the most basic level, every patron is asking, knowingly or not: "What's in this for me?" If you can successfully answer that question for them, you have made that personal connection. Personal connections can result in more broad-based support and make the library more valuable to those that the library can connect with.

We, as human beings are inherently selfish. When presented with anything new, the question in our heads is always and immediately going to be: "What's in it for ME?" When your library promotes anything, it has to answer this question clearly for the message recipients. This is how you create value in the mind of your library's patrons: by showing that value front and center.

So, think a bit differently. Every time you interact with a patron, are you connecting them to something that's truly relevant to them, or just pushing something the library hopes people will come to or do?

Just "telling people about your library's stuff" isn't enough. People need to know, plainly, what the payoff is going to be for them. If the payoff isn't clear, you're doing it wrong: there's no value proposition for the reader. Therefore, your content is, to them, useless.

Ready?

If you think you've already made this leap, from being only promotional to being actually useful, then you're cleared to move forward. If not, well . . . feel free to keep reading, but realize that you will be putting time into efforts that are unlikely to give you a good return on your investment. If you're going to put time into creating content, you might as well make the time worthwhile; create content that will do more than garner occasional comments and will help your library to meet actual goals.

I recognize that it can be very difficult to remove ego(s) from library marketing. Internal politics can derail even the best-intentioned plans. I've seen library staff get very defensive about online content they manage, when told it needed improvement. I've seen a library's administration form a public relations committee specifically to help bypass an incompetent PR manager. I've heard countless tales of "so-and-so doesn't 'get it'" from staff across the country. I suspect you might have horror tales of your own.

Collectively, libraries need to realize that online content marketing has to make this jump to maintain relevancy. Over the past decade, we've seen libraries of all types focus more tightly on concepts such as customer and user experience. The vast majority of libraries work hard to please their patrons. Online content is one area where, sadly, less progress has been made.

Let's *all* make the leap from promotional to useful.

BOTTOM LINE: Get over yourself and get the ego out of the process. Put the needs of online patrons first, just like you probably already do for them, offline. Without doing this, the rest of this book won't make much of a difference in your content marketing.

NOTES

1. Jay Baer, *Youtility: why smart marketing is about help not hype* (New York: Portfolio/Penguin, 2013).
2. Ibid.
3. Nancy R. Lee and Philip R. Kotler, *Marketing in the Public Sector: A Roadmap for Improved Performance* (Upper Saddle River, NJ: FT Press, 2006).

Should You Care About Content Marketing?
(Yeah, Probably.)

Whatever it is that you create—that's telling your story, telling people why they should hire you, why they should buy your product, rather than the competition. Content marketing has gotten very popular, it's a buzz word now. People are talking about it, because people are realizing the power of it. And if you're out there right now and you're saying well maybe that's not my business, you know, my customers are not online. That's wrong. A couple years ago, you could get away with that excuse.[1]

You don't need me to tell you that the Internet has changed everything. The ways we spend our time and our money, the ways in which we communicate, the ways in which we work . . . the world, post-Internet, has invoked massive change, on a global scale, and the impact will likely continue for decades to come.

With the advent of the Web, libraries suddenly had a new medium that they thought could be used for promotion. And, sadly, promote they do. All one has to do is look at the vast majority of social media postings, for example, to see how misguided this ideology has become. Constant streams of commands: come to this, join that, see this, check that out, get this now. Lots of mandates from libraries, usually without any justification or reasons for people to care about those mandates. Most libraries show little understanding of their audiences, or of what those audiences might want; the libraries typically shout their announcements into the online void, with the assumption that the mere act of doing so should be good enough for people to want to care about them.

This is what promotion is: the act of putting the message or the messenger first, over the potential desires of the recipient. This is why it's so important to make the cognitive leap described in chapter 1. To really make content marketing fly, you'll need to completely reverse your library's promotional mindset, and become comfortable with the idea of showing the library's value clearly, possibly only in the long term. This concept goes far beyond pushing out calls to attend programs. This means asking some new questions, about each piece of online content. These include:

+ Why does this make the library valuable to the chosen community?
+ Was this designed to meet a targeted audience's need?
+ Where can this content best serve people at their point of need?

In the past, libraries have often operated not only without asking these questions of their content, but libraries often posted online without any strategy whatsoever (and I'll address that gap in chapter 4). What happens when content marketing doesn't exist in an organization? What happens when online content is simply thrown out into the ether, with the hope that something sticks?

At the simplest level, the content fails to engage anyone. It may garner few, if any, likes or comments. However, ongoing failures can have more far-reaching consequences, such as:

+ Content continues to be ignored, because of an acquired reputation of uselessness
+ A lack of interest, or even trust, in the organization
+ The community does not value the library because the library's value has not been clearly demonstrated

Words of Wisdom from the Field
Attention Leads to Advocacy: Why Content Development Is Critical to Your Library's Future

An experienced trainer, writer, and marketing and social media strategist, Anthony Juliano approaches his work with one simple goal: to help others understand our changing communication environment. A graduate of Salem State College, Indiana University, and Indiana Tech, Anthony has nearly 20 years of experience in his field. Anthony has developed and taught college classes in social media; has presented about social media at national and international conferences; and has provided social media training for a wide variety of individuals and businesses. Anthony writes a monthly column about social media for *Greater Fort Wayne Business Weekly* and has written for a variety of publications and blogs, including *Convince and Convert*, "the world's #1 content marketing resource." He lives in Fort Wayne, Indiana, with his wife and his son.

As social media use by organizations becomes more common, it's no longer enough to simply be present. Using Facebook, Twitter, or Instagram is good start, but it merely represents the minimum effort. To truly stand out, organizations must do more. And today, the biggest differentiator is commitment to consistently sharing substantive, quality content.

Libraries may think they can sidestep this reality, assuming their audience understands that they're being asked to do more with less. Even the most ardent friend of the library, however, won't be that forgiving. If they don't get entertaining, inspiring, informative content from their local library, they'll go elsewhere—and they won't have to look very far. Over time, the organizations that secure their attention will have the greatest opportunity to secure their advocacy as well.

The irony is that few organizations are better equipped than libraries to produce attention-worthy content. Why?

FIRST, many of your people are erudite. They love language and storytelling, which is the chief skill needed to develop great content.

IN ADDITION, they likely love their library (they're probably not in it for the money, after all) and understand why others should, too. That means they're passionate—a prerequisite to getting anyone else to care about the cause.

What, then, could your content focus on? There are several options, with these being just a few examples:

BOOK REVIEWS. An obvious choice, but worth mentioning. What is your staff reading that others may find worthwhile ... or that may be overhyped?

STAFF FAVORITES. Similar to the above, but with more of a personal spin. How did reading Camus' *The Plague* affect a staff member's worldview? How was the experience of watching *The Color Purple* different in high school versus later in life? You get the idea.

AUTHOR INTERVIEWS. Conversations that give a different perspective on the books we read. Feature local authors to offer something unique.

CONTENT USEFUL TO THE AUDIENCE BEYOND BOOKS AND OTHER MEDIA. What are ten little known historical facts about your library? What are the best ways for families to spend time together at the library on a snow day? Can anyone explain—on video, in detail, with screen captures—how to borrow eBooks?

CONTENT FROM THE AUDIENCE. *Their* book reviews and favorites. What they read on vacation. Why they love the library. Get them involved in your story, and it becomes their story, too—and one they'll be much more likely to share with their friends.

The challenge in all this, of course, is that developing good content takes time and effort—which is precisely why it's such a huge factor in the overall quality of your social media strategy. It's tempting, then, to put content development into the "when I get around to it" pile or dismiss it altogether. Ask yourself this, though: *How many other options do you have to promote advocacy for your library that take time but are otherwise free?* And how likely will you be able to compete in the future if you don't secure more of your audience's attention? Instead of asking how you'll make time for content development, therefore, the real question should be what will happen if you *don't?*

BOTTOM LINE: Good content marketing has little to do with what your library wants. "There's no room for you in your marketing, only your customers"[2] —Sally Ormond, Briar Copywriting Ltd.

What Is Content Marketing, Anyway?

It's certainly not hard to find lots of information about content marketing. A Google search for "content marketing" easily brings up more than 300 million results. The same search on Amazon.com brings up more than 8,000 hits. Is it just another buzz phrase? An over-hyped fad? Unlikely. Despite the hoopla, content marketing has a solid foundation in analytics and in proven results. Content marketing has not just caught the attention of marketers in every industry:

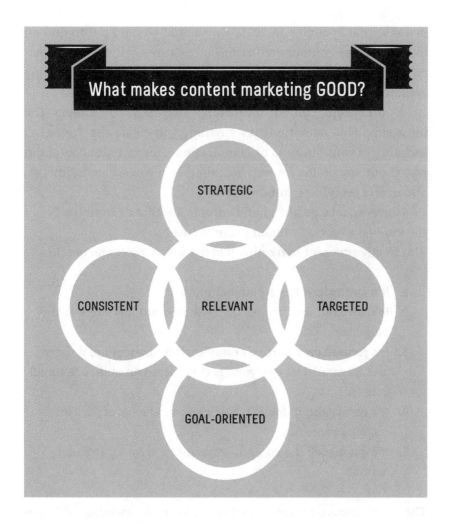

What makes content marketing GOOD?

STRATEGIC

CONSISTENT   RELEVANT   TARGETED

GOAL-ORIENTED

more importantly, it has also gotten their money. According to findings from the Content Marketing Institute, 91 percent of business-to-business marketers are using content marketing, and they are spending more of their budget on it than ever before.[3] In 2014, nonprofits spent an average of 23 percent of their marketing budgets on content marketing; 37 percent of nonprofits say they will increase that spending in 2015.[4] One would be hard put to find an industry where content marketing budgets are not increasing. Obviously, marketing professionals feel strongly that content marketing is more than just a fad.

As a concept, content marketing is actually very simple. The most simplified definition? It's anything you create that helps tell the story of your business or organization. This includes content in just about any online format, including blog posts, videos, images, and nearly everything in-between.

However, let's go ahead and complicate that definition a bit, in the interest of actually making it more useful.

Effective content marketing has the following characteristics:[5]

1. **It's strategic:** it has a plan behind it.
2. **It's relevant:** the content being shared out has value to the audience.
3. **It's focused on a particular audience:** audiences are defined and targeted. Not everyone is considered an audience for all content.
4. **It's consistent:** it doesn't "just happen whenever;" it's an ongoing process.
5. **It's got a goal:** the content is meant to drive a particular action.

There's an important difference between *content marketing* and *information* that you'll need to be especially clear on: *information* doesn't bother with being relevant. When your library simply posts about a forthcoming program, ignoring the need to make that post valuable to the audience, that's information, and these days it's generally a waste of time. People no longer have attention available for merely perusing what they see. They scan, quickly, looking for those things that have immediate application to *them*. Remember the payoff from chapter 1: that's the real difference between information and content marketing . . . and between failing and succeeding.

> **BOTTOM LINE:** Content marketing's strength (and the reason so many organizations are now using it so heavily) is because it does not just shove information at people. The focus is on the created content being useful and valuable.

How Is Content Marketing Different from Content Promotion?

When it comes to content, it may be difficult to see what makes promotion different from marketing. Even the words "promotion" and "marketing" are sometimes used interchangeably, making the delineation even harder. However, more recently, marketing professionals have become increasingly clear about where the border actually lies.

Alex Sobal, of the Weidert Group marketing agency, uses a great analogy to help explain.[6] Suppose you are planning a birthday party for a friend. To get people to come to the party, you tweet about the party and post flyers around town. This is content promotion: it's not directed at anyone in particular.

To make it more likely that people will show up to the party, you send out individual invitations to the people your friend would most like to see at the birthday celebration. This is content marketing: the audience is defined. "Rather than sharing the post with everyone and hoping for as much engagement as possible, you send your content to a specific person or list of people. You're very targeted with your approach, and you're very careful about making sure the right contacts get the right content."[7]

Promotion vs. Marketing

PROMOTION

- Tweeting announcement of new book being available
- Posting a link for an upcoming program on Facebook
- Creating a video showing a patron happily using a database

MARKETING

- A series of tweets, describing one book
- Sending an e-mail to specific patrons, building anticipation
- Creating a video clearly showing real uses of a database

When you are promoting something, you are merely telling people that it exists. You are telling them what. When you are marketing something, you are showing people its value. You are telling them why.
—TwoPlus Media

Libraries (especially public ones) have traditionally had ongoing struggles with wanting to be all things to all people. Most libraries serve all kinds of people and very diverse communities; targeting a particular audience can seem like a very foreign concept. For your content marketing efforts to take hold though, you'll need to shift how you think about who gets which content. (We'll discuss identifying and targeting audiences more in chapter 3.) No more throwing whatever is handy at the virtual wall, to see what sticks.

Libraries have long tried to promote themselves, their collections and their services, without understanding that promotion doesn't demonstrate value; promotion only provides information to a broad base of users. By changing efforts to focus on marketing, less effort is wasted and results are likely to improve.

BOTTOM LINE: Content promotion is about the library. Content marketing is about the library's value to the patron.

Why Does Your Library Need to Start Focusing on Content Marketing?

As discussed in the last section, content marketing is about proving the worth of your library to its patrons. Let's be honest: this is harder work than merely posting announcements online. It's going to take more thought, planning, and drive than you may previously have devoted to your library's online presence. Many libraries already struggle with just getting *anything* up online. Why bother going the extra mile?

1. *Change perception.*
Keep in mind that valuable content has a much more long-lasting impact on readers. Useful information gets

bookmarked, liked, commented upon, and shared. It can change the perception of the library in the long term; the library becomes a resource, a utility, that is relevant. Libraries have always been relevant and good resources for almost any kind of pursuit. However, they struggle to show that more than ever in this digital era. How many times have you heard statements like, "Who needs the library, when I've got Google?" By creating content that gets more word-of-mouth exposure, a library can help people recognize the library's worth.

2. Improve search rankings.
You may already be aware that Google is always fine-tuning its search algorithm and rankings. Over the past several years, Google has updated these to increase the rankings of content that it deems is more authoritative. This not only helps to prevent companies from "gaming" search results in their favor, but serves to make search a better experience for users. On top of these changes, Google has also instituted a process called AuthorRank, which prioritizes the content of individual, reputable authors.

What does this mean for libraries? It means that getting your library's content to come up in a search for anything beyond actually searching for the name of the institution is going to be more difficult.

If someone is doing a Google search for "library" and your location or institution, your library is still likely to come up in the first page of results. However, what if a user is searching for "tax assistance?" If you're a public library, you probably have at least some paper forms, and possibly local volunteers coming in to help seniors prepare their tax returns. You may even have posted about these things online. That, however, is not enough for Google to take notice. On the other hand, if your library provided a blog post (possibly written by a tax volunteer) about common tax mistakes to avoid, that content may be valuable and have further reach than an announcement about having tax forms. That post may be shared on various social networks, resulting in a potentially higher ranking by Google. The search engine giant's algorithm much prefers content that is popular, as it takes popularity into account when deciding the authoritativeness factor. If something is useful, it's chances of being popular increase significantly . . . as well as its chances of being seen by Google.

3. Advertising can't do the job any more.
In the online realm, trust is of utmost importance. Advertising, which has been around for decades, falls down on the job when used online. The principal reason for this revolves around how people often use the Internet. Instead of waiting to be told about things, people are proactively gathering information on their own. They're checking with their peers to get recommendations. When they have a need, they actively search for information needed to fulfill it, and they usually check with a trusted resource for reviews and answers. Advertising is not usually viewed as a trusted source online, so purely promotional posts become nearly useless. Word-of-mouth marketing has always been valuable, but the nature of how people use the web makes that value increasingly significant. "Being encouraged and reassured by a trusted source has more value than any other sort of advertising."[8]

If a library wants to have a meaningful presence, it's going to have to build trust and rapport—something that promotional content just can't do.

BOTTOM LINE: If your library wants to be a valuable resource in its given community, online, it's going to have to prove it via content marketing. Promotional posts do not build the necessary trust to change perception.

NOTES

1. C.C. Chapman, "Introduction to Content Marketing," Lynda.com course.
2. Sally Ormond, "This Is Why Content Marketing Is Important," January 22, 2015, www.briarcopywriting.com/blog/this-is-why-content-marketing-is-important/.
3. Copyblogger, "Content Marketing: How to Build an Audience that Builds Your Business," www.copyblogger.com/content-marketing/.
4. Content Marketing Institute, "2015 Nonprofit Content Marketing: Benchmarks, Budgets, and Trends—North America," http://contentmarketinginstitute.com/wp-content/uploads/2014/11/2015_NonProf_Research.pdf.
5. Content Marketing Institute, "What Is Content Marketing?: Useful content should be at the core of your marketing," http://contentmarketinginstitute.com/what-is-content-marketing/.
6. Alex Sobal, "The Difference Between Content Promotion and Content Distribution," December 22, 2014, www.weidert.com/whole_brain_marketing_blog/the-difference-between-content-promotion-and-content-distribution.
7. Ibid.
8. Entrepreneur, "Why Influencer Marketing Pays Off for Small Businesses," February 27, 2015, http://finance.yahoo.com/news/why-influencer-marketing-pays-off-230000605.html;_ylt=A0LEVjgQVPNUH3IAmSslnIlQ.

Identifying Your Audience(s)

"Aim for allies, not fans."
—Chris Brogan, CEO of Owner Media Group[1]

Ideally, you've already begun to understand the need to shift how your library thinks about what it does online. This book has (hopefully) made it clear that just posting online, for the sake of having done so, is a method that has no real value for your library in the long term. However, the move from content promotion to content marketing is only the first transformation your library's methodology has to undergo, in order to be successful.

Libraries (especially public ones) are about providing services to many different populations. As library staff, we often want to help as many people, in as many different ways, as possible. While this is admirable, it's hardly realistic, particularly when resources and time are limited commodities. Your library may have had to make some decisions about where to focus those resources; perhaps a poorly attended program on local history was canceled, in favor of a program geared to helping job seekers. Maybe your library has found its series of bibliographies, booklists, or pathfinders is not well used, and decided to discontinue them. Libraries, of all types, have to make choices like this all the time. We would like to provide services and materials to everyone we might serve, but we know that isn't a pragmatic approach . . . no matter how much we might desire it to be otherwise. Libraries have to be careful with their resources, and be able to justify how they are used. Services that they provide also have to be sound returns on their patrons' investments.

When posting content online, it can be very, very easy to forget that these same kinds of decisions still have to be made. The audience is literally out of sight, so we're not always sure just whom we're serving. Engagement with posts can be low or negligible if the effort that is put into posting by the library is slight or is using poor practices. Statistics can be difficult to interpret—if staff even takes the time to look at them. It's no wonder that so many libraries just throw things out into the ether, figuratively speaking. Doing anything else takes yet more effort and isn't simple.

BOTTOM LINE: Actually figuring out what to post and to whom it should be geared isn't going to be as easy as just guessing. Shift your thinking to making the best possible effort with the resources available: return on investment is critical.

Focus on the Right Thing

Before you dive into this process, take a minute and remind your-self about *why* it's so important to go through it. It can be too easy to get caught up in the idea of increasing traffic, when what we really want to do with content marketing is increase relevance. Jus-tin Gray, CEO & chief marketing evangelist of LeadMD, says: ". . . all the pretty and witty creative in the world isn't going to hook your audience unless the message actually matters to them. Yet some-how, teams keep making that classic mistake. *They focus on what they want to say, rather than what their buyers want to hear.*"[2]

Gray's statement is a stark reminder that too much, online, is written to appeal to the marketer, not the reader. This is directly contrary to catering to specific audiences, because creating content this way means that the audience is the marketer.

Let's face it: writing for ourselves is a piece of cake. Writing for others? Not so much.

Figuring out which audiences you should be spending time on isn't the most glamorous part of any content marketer's job. Envi-sioning new campaigns or infographics is probably more appealing. But, none of the other, more "fun" stuff will matter if it isn't relevant to anyone. Whatever you do create is likely to be ignored, and *that* isn't fun at all. It can make you feel unappreciated, if not outright incompetent.

I've never met anyone in any library, ever, who didn't have more than enough work to do. Unless you are the exception, don't waste your time. Before you spend any time writing blog posts, cre-ating visuals, or counting characters in tweets, you need to know to whom you're talking.

Mark W. Schaefer, in his 2015 book *The Content Code*, introduces the idea of "Content Shock." The amount of freely available online content has exploded, with no slowing down in the near future. He says that we should expect around a 500 percent estimated increase in web content in the next five years. If people are feeling overwhelmed now, imagine how bad it's going get by the year 2020. People already consume an average of 10 hours a day, according to Schaefer. What happens when the amount of available content continues to rise at a staggering rate?

This crossroads, between what people can actually manage to consume and the exponential rate of content creation, is what Schaefer means when he coined the term "Content Shock." The supply of online content is only increasing, but our ability to consume it isn't. In this environment, trying to get attention for your content is going to get way, way harder. There are simply too many things competing for attention, and the situation is only going to get worse, not better.

The information density on the Web is taking standard marketing practices and quickly making them obsolete. There's simply too much noise for people to hear many individual signals. At all. This is perhaps the most important reason for figuring out who your real targets are going to be. When it is so incredibly difficult just to have any content seen, libraries cannot afford to just guess about what to post.

BOTTOM LINE: Libraries serve people, and they can't serve people well unless they understand who those people are. There's just too darned much content on the Web for a library to guess what will work; a data-driven strategy is fast becoming the only path to getting eyeballs on your library's content.

Who Is the *Real* Audience?

If you understand the need to focus on specific groups, then you know that the next step is to pinpoint which groups those are. This process doesn't have to be as complex as you might think. Either you, or the staff of your library, probably already has a pretty good idea about some possible broad categories. For example, if your library is an academic one, the immediate groups that come to mind might include:

+ Faculty
+ Staff
+ Students

These are groups; however, collectively, these are patrons by role and don't necessarily constitute content audiences. You need to move beyond just a role or job title, and dig a little deeper (I know, yet more effort is going to be involved). You're going to need to make another shift, now. Gray says that marketers need to understand people's triggers and goals.[3] What are their needs? What do they want? What are their interests? What are their pain points? Which emotions can you appeal to? Obviously, at least some of the questions will span more than one patron category.

So, it's time to do a little research. You're going to need to do what's sometimes referred to as an audience assessment. This will give you more information about who your audience is, and what potential groups you might want to gear your content towards. It will show you how your patrons seek information, how they evaluate what they find and even how they might make decisions. Public relations firm Relevance lists several methods for conducting an assessment, four of which are good fits for libraries:[4]

Keyword research. By identifying keywords and related search terms that your patrons use when searching, it can boost understanding of their needs. Are your patrons constantly searching for "bestsellers" or "how to fix a broken pipe?" Ideally, you'll be able to get this information from your library's catalog and/or website. Armed with this information, it can not only help with generating user personas (which is discussed in the next section), but can help your library do smart content marketing. Having a list of keywords, popular with your patrons, is almost like having a "Write About This Stuff to Be Successful" list. You'll also want to explore what's trending on the Web, using Google Trends (www.google.com/trends) or a tool like Buzzsumo (http://buzzsumo.com/), which I'll cover in chapter 4.

User-generated content analysis. Look at blogs and social media that your patrons produce, or look at the comments they make on what your library does. Examine how people in your community interact online with local organizations and businesses. This kind of audit can tell you some important things: what people want, what kinds of problems they have, and what kind of terminology they use. Are people in your community complaining about not finding good nannies, or potholes in the roads? Are students upset because the campus coffee shop closes too early? When people do say things online, are they using a lot of acronyms? How casual is the language? You can also get a general idea of where your audience might be, online. Are local Instagram accounts much more active than local Facebook pages? All of these kinds of data points can help piece together a better picture of your audience.

Customer interviews and surveys. This is especially valuable to do after user-generated content analysis. Directly contacting patrons can help to solidify the picture you may have started piecing together with the content analysis. It may seem that everyone was complaining about the coffee shop closing early, but perhaps that was just a vocal few on a particular social channel, and is not a pain point that can be generalized to an entire group. The idea is to connect the data you get from interviews and surveys with patrons to data you have gotten from other methods.

Web analytics assessment. Yes, you need analytics to measure success (and we'll cover that in a later chapter), but you need them at the front end of this process, also. Your website's analytics can help you to gain a clearer understanding of the demographics that may use your library and how they interact with your library's website. They can also help you to figure out how to better use existing content. Some of your library's current content may be able to be repurposed somewhere else, for a different population.

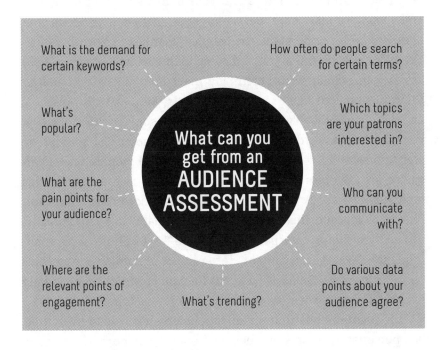

BOTTOM LINE: Don't guess about who your audience really is. There is data out there; go get it. To do otherwise is to waste time and resources.

Creating Personas

One of the most common ways to categorize content audiences is by creating marketing personas. This is not a single user; rather, it is a profile of a particular group of users and their likely characteristics. By figuring out some probable personas, you can better determine what kinds of marketing may appeal to certain groups. Personas can help guide future decisions about your library's content marketing and allow for much more precise targeting. They can also help your library to better understand the people it is interacting with online.

By knowing more about and categorizing users' behaviors, your library can plan how to potentially meet their needs and answer their questions. If one of your personas is "Mother with preschool age child," you probably already know at least some of the things that you might aim towards that group. Information about age-appropriate story times, the toy lending library, and how to prepare for kindergarten are all topics geared specifically for this persona. Maybe this group uses Facebook heavily, and so using Facebook to get this information to this audience would be the ideal channel. If your library is an academic library, one persona might be "Last-Minute Assignment Student." Kevan Lee, a content crafter at social media sharing company Buffer, says: "Building personas for your core audience can help improve the way you solve problems for your customers."[5]

Lee recommends that organizations create three to five different personas to represent their audience. That numeric range is broad enough to cover most of the user base, while not being so large that efforts will be spread too thinly. There is a plethora of free templates on the Web for creating content marketing personas, but most will have the something like the following items, as described by Kentico Marketing:[6]

+ What is the segments' age range?
+ What is the segment's educational level?
+ What is the segment's social interest?
+ What is the segment's job status?
+ What is the segment's typical work experience?
+ Where is the segment likely to get their information? (TV, Internet, Facebook, LinkedIn, Twitter, etc.)?
+ What three adjectives would the segment use to describe themselves?

Additional characteristics might also include more demographic information, such as gender or location. Some more helpful criteria, found on many templates, may be to specify the segment's goals and challenges. Noting how your library can help the persona meet these can really help to fine-tune content marketing. The library can use the goals and challenges of each persona as a way to drive content creation; if content doesn't meet the needs of any particular persona, it's unlikely to be successful. Again, remember that effectiveness is almost completely dependent on relevance. If the content doesn't somehow solve a problem for anyone, it's often a waste of time. Developing marketing personas saves time for your library in the long run, while increasing the odds that the entire content marketing endeavor is on track.

Persona creation can also differ from industry to industry, so you may want to include additional information. Even interviewing people face-to-face, to help create personas, can be helpful. What blogs do they read? Where do they get their news? What are their hobbies? How comfortable are they with different kinds of technology? The answers to these kinds of questions can help flesh out your marketing personas and potentially spur content development. Don't forget that, if you've done an audience assessment already, all of the information you collected will be the ideal foundation for creating these personas.

Words of Wisdom from the Field
Going beyond the Demographics

Paula Watson-Lakamp is the communications manager for Poudre River Public Library District in Fort Collins, Colorado, and has been in this position for 8 years. Paula has a background in communications, marketing, special events, graphic design, brand management, and social media, and has owned her own marketing and design business and worked for nonprofits and city governments for the last 25 years. She is author of the book *Marketing Moxie for Librarians—Fresh Ideas, Proven Techniques, and Innovative Approaches*, published by Libraries Unlimited.

Using only demographic data for your target or segmented audience no longer works. Because libraries often need to have something for everyone, using your customer demographics along with ethnographic snapshots, surveys, focus groups, and any other tools you can find out who they are, is important to claiming their "personas." Using customer-focused personas to segment who you are delivering your services to and building that personal relationship with them is what every marketer is looking for. An easy way to think of these segments is to come up with personas for four imaginary friends. These might be your neighbors, or your children's best friends. When writing your content, try to emphasize what is important to them; identify their interests, how they like to get their information, as well as what information would be applicable to their lives. Doing this also helps your content to be customer-focused. As an exercise, here are some questions to answer about your imaginary friends. Write down their name, gender, income, age, job title, and where they live, Go beyond those demographics and write down what concerns them about the community, what their aspirations are, and what their biggest need is. Are they busy two-parent working families who need convenience, teens who need somewhere to escape to, or older adults looking for valuable ways to spend their time? Then add whether they are library users or nonusers. If they are users, how do they use the library? Do they check out print materials only, mainly check out eBooks, come to the library to use the Wi-Fi or computers, or come to programs but never check anything out? Basically, list their library behaviors. Thinking of these personas while you are writing your content will make it much easier not only to write, but to market to those people.

Our library district, which is made up of three libraries serving a population of 180,000, hired the firm OrangeBoy, Inc. to help us discover our customers and their library behaviors. OrangeBoy, Inc. identifies customer behaviors through its market segmentation clustering algorithm within their Savannah system. After using surveys (both online and paper), an onsite ethnographic survey, and pulling data from various circulation statistics, market analysis, and a cardholder assessment, they were able to sort our customers into eleven "clusters." These cluster groups ranged from the "Occasionals," who are cardholders that read, but not a lot—they stop by the library infrequently and we compete for their business with online store, and local bookshops—to the "Dependables," who are at the opposite end of the spectrum—they are the folks who visit the library a few times a month, enjoy books, DVDs, programs, and everything else the library has to offer. They place holds via the website catalog and can be found browsing shelves for additional materials after they pick up their holds. They almost always use the library as their sole source for materials they enjoy. Additional cluster groups included the Bedtime Stories (families with young children), the Double Features (people who ravage the DVD section), the Digitarians (patrons who manage their library habits through their smartphone or other digital device), and many more. These cluster groupings can contain different ages, incomes, races, etc., and are focused on library behaviors that a marketer can use to segment not only your message, but the way you relay that message to be received by your intended audience.

Building relationships with your customers in this way helps to give you a more customer-focused content creation plan as well as contextual data that you can access over time to track trends and changes in your customer base.

BOTTOM LINE: To really do content marketing right, your library is going to have to buckle down and figure out who's reading the content, and what they need. Personas give you a way to actually target content.

NOTES

1. Mark W. Schaefer, *The Content Code* (Mark W. Schaefer, 2015).
2. Justin Gray, "How to Drill Down to Your True Target Audience," www.convinceandconvert.com/social-media-strategy/how-to-drill-down -to-your-true-target-audience/.
3. Ibid.
4. Relevance, "Quick Guide for Content Marketing Research: The 4 Essential Research Assessments," http://digital.relevance.com/hubfs/Quick_Guide_for _Content_Marketing_Research.pdf.
5. Kevan Lee, "Marketing Personas: The Complete Beginner's Guide," March 27, 2014, https://blog.bufferapp.com/marketing-personas-beginners-guide.
6. Kentico Marketing, "Quick Start Guide: Marketing Persona," https://www .kentico.com/Product/Resources/Quick-Start-Guides/Kentico-Marketing -Personas-Quick-Start-Guide/Marketing-Personas.

Planning Not to Fail

"If you fail to plan, you are planning to fail."
—Benjamin Franklin

If you are reading this book, your library has probably had mixed results from its online content. Some things might get some engagement, while perhaps many others are just completely ignored. That's the norm for many libraries (and even businesses and other kinds of organizations). There will always be some content that does better than other content.

However, it's likely that you've noticed that the balance of successful posts to those that are bypassed isn't in your library's favor. In this new era of content shock, it's extremely difficult to make content effective; and, in the majority of cases, libraries don't have any kind of real plan in place for improving their content marketing.

In this case, libraries are not alone. A 2015 study found that only 12 percent of businesses have an optimized content marketing strategy.[1] Which, when one thinks about it, is a rather stunning statistic, when you consider another piece of data, found by the same study: 71 percent of businesses will create more content in 2015 than in 2014. So: the majority of online entities are probably creating *more* content than ever before, but only a small number of those actually have bothered to plan to do it successfully. With some proactive thinking and effort, your library can break from the pack and make its content marketing stand out.

Start with the Goals

So many libraries simply create content for the sake of creating content. Often, they find themselves in situations similar to "OK, I know I have to post *something* today . . . what should I post about?" Not only does this show a planning deficit, it also demonstrates a lack of understanding. This is entirely the wrong question to be asking.

Before your library starts creating any content, it's going to need to take a long, hard look at *why* it's posting anything at all. Successful content finds the intersection of your library's goals and those of your readers. If your library has gone through the process to define target audiences (see chapter 3 for more on this), it also has to figure out what the real goals of the library are. Only then can it calculate what kinds of content will be at that juncture of the library's needs and those of the audience.

Some libraries have separate goals for their plans, but often one of the easiest ways to list content marketing goals (and perhaps the most integrated marketing approach) is to use those already laid out in your library's overall strategic plan. Using this method also helps to better tie marketing efforts to everything else going on at the library. Marketing of any kind is not a separate endeavor from what your library does; rather, it is meant to help strengthen the ties with its community and show its value very clearly to stakeholders.

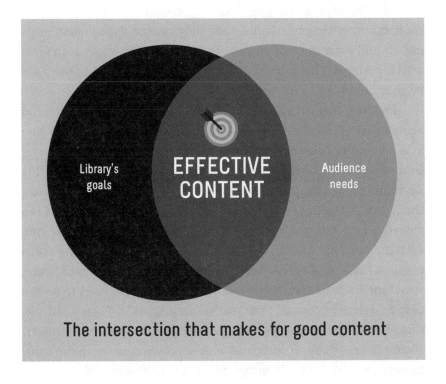

Library's goals

EFFECTIVE CONTENT

Audience needs

The intersection that makes for good content

When your library plans a post (more about this part of the process will be covered later in this chapter), it should, ideally, be able to point back to a specific goal. If your library is posting about "5 Things You Didn't Know You Could Do with XYZ Online Database," it should be clearly connected to the strategic goals laid out in your library's content marketing plan. If your library decides to post about a craft program, to which goal is that tied? If it's simply a fun program to keep kids busy, it might not be something worthy of an online post. On the other hand, if it's a story time, perhaps that can be tied to a library goal of encouraging early literacy, or getting ready for kindergarten. Or, if the craft program includes some kind of literacy component, perhaps it would be worth a post.

Some library staff may be discouraged by the need to constantly connect content to goals. Some staff enjoy spur-of-the-moment posting. Should every piece of content be connected to a goal? In an ideal world, perhaps. This is a policy decision that will need to be made by your library's administration.

However, there is something to be said for being flexible and being able to post something at a moment's notice, especially when it is something that captures the zeitgeist of a very recent event. Oreo cookies became one of the most talked about examples of this flexibility, during the 2013 Super Bowl. While a power outage caused the lights in the Superdome to go out for over half an hour, Oreo posted a now-famous image of a lone, dimly lit cookie on Twitter, with the caption "You can still dunk in the dark."[2] Advertising agencies and marketers everywhere praised the timely reflexes of Oreo's social media team, and the move was widely considered to be the best ad-related event of that year's Super Bowl. A library can use this same of-the-moment posting when, for example, a well-known author passes away, or some major event on campus or in the community can be effectively integrated in a timely way.

Connecting goals to your library's content, and making that part of your strategy, also helps define internally what kinds of content are created or prioritized. It gives you a foundation for why certain kinds of things are not posted or promoted. Angela Hursh, content team leader, Marketing Department at Public Library of Cincinnati and Hamilton County, says that a strategy can also provide "a concrete reason the next time you have to say that small and yet very important word . . . 'no.' Say 'no' to promotions that don't serve to drive your library's strategic mission."[3]

BOTTOM LINE: Don't post stuff just to post stuff. The content that your library creates should tie directly into at least one of the library's strategic goals. Marketing expert Jay Baer says: "Content helps achieve business objectives, not content objectives."[4]

Evaluate What You Already Have

At this point, it's unlikely that your library has absolutely no online content at all; it's almost certainly not starting from scratch. Perhaps it has various social media channels, a blog and/or a digital newsletter. There may be informational posts on the library's website. All of these are examples of existing content, and your next step is to figure out what content you already have at your disposal and connect it with some important, associated information. It's time to do a content audit.

A content audit is a good way to chart and to evaluate existing content for various criteria. It allows you to objectively analyze and collect facts about your content, and look closely at its strengths and weaknesses. What's still relevant, and what isn't? Typically, it consists of a spreadsheet, with rows for each piece of content and many columns to be filled out for each piece. There are many templates that can freely be found on the Web, but most will at least include most or all of the following criteria:

+ URL
+ Title

+ General topic
+ Images being used
+ Date last updated
+ Content condition (still relevant or not)
+ Type of content (blog post, video, photo, etc.)
+ Author
+ Owner (Who is responsible for editing it now?)
+ Number of likes, comments, social shares
+ Number of visits, average time on page
+ Does it support the library's goals?

Let's be clear here, though—this is not going to be a fun or quick project. (I know . . . nothing so far has been easy!) Doing an audit is, admittedly, time-consuming. Don't let this deter you. Doing a full audit will give you a clearer picture of where you are and where you need to go. Don't be tempted to do just a quick scan. "Conducting a 'quick' content audit is like trying to figure out why your car won't start by glancing at the paint,[5]" says Anthony Gaenzle, founder and lead strategist at AG Integrated Marketing Strategists. You need to come up with a document that will be the foundation of your content marketing plan, and you don't want to be building on shaky ground.

Your first task will be to create a spreadsheet (or use an existing template) to list all of your current content assets. If there are simply too many assets or posts to be examined, you may want to limit the list to just those from the past year or two. Also, doing this for every social media post may not be practical. You may want to also limit the number further, but try to keep the minimum to three months' worth, so that you can get a real feel for any recent trends.

The second task, after filling out the audit spreadsheet, is to evaluate what you have. Assign a score to each asset. You can decide a scoring system for yourself, but using a school-like "A to F" grade is fairly common. Items with a high grade are those that are top-performing, while those with low grades probably should be removed, or at the least, probably not used going forward or as inspiration for future content.

Once these tasks are completed, it's time to start analyzing.

One last note about content audits. The marketing team at Singlegrain.com says, "Realistically, you're never going to be working

NAVIGATION TITLE		FILES	LAST UPDATED	OWNER	COMMENTS	DELETE?	OVERALL GRADE
0.0	HOME		09/24/15	Marketing	Too much text		C
1.0	ABOUT US		?	?	Who is maintaining this section?		B
1.1	History		02/16/13		Do we have any old photos to include?		C
1.2	Board of Trustees		06/05/15		Add photos of board members		B
1.3	Hours & Location		?		Add building photo		B
1.4	Mission Statement		?		Include examples of mission in action		B
1.5	Policies		?		Needs other policies added		C
1.5.1	Code of conduct		05/11/14				A
1.5.2	Computer use		05/13/14				A
1.6	Staff		?		Needs updating		D
2.0	RESEARCH		03/22/15	Adult Services	Change the name to "Find Information"		B
2.1	Research databases		08/30/15		Need to better categorize & explain benefits		D
2.2	Recommended websites		08/29/15		Rarely used except by staff	Y	F
2.3	Local history & genealogy	6 PDF files	10/22/15		Break out to own top-level option?		A
3.0	SERVICES			Marketing			B
3.1	Computer classes		09/10/15		Needs direct links to programs		C
3.2	Faxing & copying		08/17/13				A
3.3	Meeting rooms	1 PDF file	08/17/13		Need photos/diagrams		B
4.0	LATEST NEWS		?	Marketing	No content on page—news is on homepage	Y	F
5.0	EVENTS		n/a	n/a	Links directly to calendar		A
6.0	CONTACT US		n/a	n/a	Address, phone, email address & contact form		A

with perfect information, in a perfect environment."[6] You have to work with what you have and do the best you can. Even experts can't always make great predictions based on the data collected in an audit. However, doing an audit is still far more beneficial than not, and will enable you to make clearer choices when determining your library's content marketing strategy.

BOTTOM LINE: Don't skip the content audit. Even if your data isn't perfect, audits allow you to create your content strategy on a much stronger foundation.

Planning Ahead: The Editorial Calendar

If you're one of the staff responsible for your library's content marketing, it's probably a safe bet that, at some point, you've been at a loss trying to figure out what to post. It happens to everyone, eventually. An editorial calendar can cut down on the number of times this happens (or even eliminate being stumped for ideas—at the last minute—completely).

Journals and magazines have long used editorial calendars to help them plan what will be in each issue. They help publishers to visualize their content planning in a chronological way. A content marketing editorial calendar does the same thing, but is often much more strategic and detailed than a print publication version. You are creating a planning document that will be part of the core foundation of your content marketing work. It is an essential best practice that, once you have completed the first one, will make you wonder how you lived without it.

You may have eyed editorial calendars before and thought: "These look *way* too complicated!" Granted, some can get very extensive, and there's even specialized software available to create and manage content marketing calendars. Fortunately, since libraries typically are not trying to manage marketing to millions of people and/or across the globe, there's usually no call for them to need anything beyond a simple system. Some use Google Docs or Google Calendar, some use spreadsheets. And, yes, there are also plenty of freely available templates to be found with a simple online search. Whichever system works for you is the one you should use.

Start by listing all of your content types. List your library's blog(s), video series, website(s), and any regular e-mail newsletters. If your library produces ebooks, events, or webinars, include those also. (Note that we're not talking about social media channels, like Facebook or Twitter, yet. Those are more for content distribution, not generally for creation.) For each, you're going to have to make some decisions about how often you can create content for each type. You might be feeling very enthusiastic, and believe that you're going to create new content every day, or even multiple times per day. While this ambition is admirable, it may not be practical, especially over time. Consider how often your library can truly support posting; if that's only one blog post a week, that's OK. If sending an e-mail newsletter more than once per month isn't a reasonable expectation, don't assume you'll do more. Many people mistakenly believe that online content is "free" to create, and that simply isn't true. There is always going to be a cost in staff time, and that has to be accounted for. Be realistic; you can always add more content later. Also consider that your library will likely post things outside of what's planned on the editorial calendar; having that flexibility allows it to respond to external events and take advantage of "of the moment" content. The number of times you plan to create a particular content type should be the minimum, and you should plan for those accordingly.

The next step is to figure out what will be created. This is the heart of the editorial calendar, because it removes any last-minute panic and allows you to be strategic with what gets posted. This is also where your content audit will be a solid guide; you'll have an idea of what kinds of content have (and have not) worked before. Ideally, you should match a topic to a content type. Some topics will lend themselves better, say, to a blog post, while others might be better suited to a series of photos. How detailed you get is up to you: some organizations simply list a broad topic, while others will create the exact headline to be used. Many organizations use a series of themes, either by week or by month, around which they write their posts. For some, having a theme for a period of time makes content creation easier. Plan your topics or headlines for at least two or three months in advance.

Be very careful of simply looking at your library's event or program calendar, and using that as the solitary basis for your editorial calendar. This approach can quickly devolve into becoming nothing but promotion after promotion. It also will result in content with very little diversity. More importantly, posting nothing but promotional material often violates Jay Baer's notion of "Youtility." Whatever content your library posts has to show its value clearly. This can certainly be done with some posts about your library's events but, at some point, readers will realize how self-serving the content is and begin to tune out.

As you develop your editorial calendar, you'll need to include not just the content itself, but to which channels it will be distributed, and how often. Some refer to this as a social sharing calendar.

This is where social media channels come in. In most content marketing, social media is used to distribute other content and is not considered the content itself. As you have probably already guessed, some content will lend itself better to some social media than others. If your library takes photographs of its newly arrived furniture, those photographs can be distributed across a variety of channels: Instagram, Facebook, or Flickr, just to name a possible few. A blog post, on the other hand, might be better broken down into some choice tweets, or as a teaser on Facebook.

It is vital that a piece of content be shared more than once. People will not necessarily catch it the first time it appears on a channel; seeing something more than once also may increase the chances of some action being taken by the viewer. Nathan Ellering, from the company CoSchedule. shares these time periods that they use for their social sharing calendar:[7]

+ On publish
+ Same day as post
+ Day after post
+ Week after post
+ Month after post
+ Custom date

One piece of content may be shared on different channels, multiple times. However, be sure to vary the wording. Don't share the same message too often, or your sharing becomes spam.

The absolute minimum criteria for your educational calendar include the content type, the topic/headline, and when and how often the content will be shared. To make it even more effective, however, some other columns should be added:

+ Which audience (persona) is this content targeting?
+ Which strategic goal is this content serving?

By including these two criteria as well, you ensure that your content is on track with your library's overall goals.

WEEK OF: August 3–9 **THEME:** Starting kindergarten **STRATEGIC GOAL:** Encourage early literacy

DAY OF WEEK	CONTENT TOPIC	CONTENT TYPE	AUDIENCE	f	◉	✦
MONDAY	List of books about starting kindergarten	Blog post	Parents with small children	• On publish • 3 days after publish	N/A	• On publish • Same day as post • Day after post • Week after post
TUESDAY	Special "Going to Kindergarten" story time	Event	Parents with small children	• One week before registration opens • When registration opens • Day before registration closes	• One week before registration opens • When registration opens • Day before registration closes	• One week before registration opens • When registration opens • Every other day until registration closes
WEDNESDAY						
THURSDAY	Kindergarten readiness websites	Email newsletter	Parents with small children	• On publish • Week after post	N/A	• On publish • Day after post • Week after post
FRIDAY	Best educational apps for young kids	Blog post	Parents with small children	• On publish • Month after post	• On publish • Month after post	• On publish • Day after post • Week after post • Month after post
SATURDAY/ SUNDAY	Funny "Things You Need for Kindergarten" video by Childeren's Services	Video	Parents with small children	• On publish • Week after post	• On publish	• On publish • Week after post

DATE	CONTENT	SEGMENT	PLATFORM
Sunday, February 1, 2015	Promoting African American Heritage Month	everyone	Facebook, Twitter, Google +
Wednesday, February 4, 2015	Promoting semester long graphing calculator loans	students	Facebook, Twitter, Google +
Thursday, February 5, 2015	Photos from the library exhibit	students & faculty	Instagram (syndicates on Facebook)
Saturday, February 7, 2015	Launching of the new Technology Support Center	everyone	Facebook, Twitter, Google +
Sunday, February 8, 2015	Promoting the Freedom Riders exhibit	students & faculty	Facebook, Twitter, Google +
Tuesday, February 10, 2015	Promoting Library workshops for First Year Students	first year students	Facebook, Twitter, Google +

DATE	CONTENT	SEGMENT	PLATFORM
Wednesday, February 11, 2015	Promoting Freedom Riders exhibit by NY1 interview of librarian	students & faculty	Facebook, Twitter, Google +
Wednesday, February 11, 2015	Information, not a promotional post	everyone	Facebook, Twitter, Google +
Friday, February 13, 2015	Images of new books	everyone	Instagram (syndicates on Facebook)
Friday, February 13, 2015	Introducing our new mousepads	everyone	Instagram (syndicates on Facebook)
Monday, February 16, 2015	Information, not a promotional post	students & faculty	Facebook, Twitter, Google +
Monday, February 23, 2015	Promote new database eMarketer	students & faculty	Facebook, Twitter, Google +
Tuesday, February 24, 2015	Promote Freedom Riders Exhibit and Discussion (CLUE credit)	students & faculty	Facebook, Twitter, Google +
Monday, March 2, 2015	Promote Women's History Month womenshistorymonth.gov	students & faculty	Facebook, Twitter, Google +
Tuesday, March 3, 2015	Promote library exhibit	students & faculty	Facebook, Twitter, Google +
Thursday, March 5, 2015	Information, not a promotional post	students & faculty	Facebook, Twitter, Google +
Saturday, March 7, 2015	Promote library exhibit	students, faculty, general public	Facebook, Twitter, Google +
Monday, March 9, 2015	Photos from the library exhibit	students, faculty, general public	Instagram (syndicates on Facebook)
Wednesday, March 11, 2015	Promote a new database	students & faculty	Facebook, Twitter, Google +
Friday, March 13, 2015	Promote streaming video	students & faculty	Facebook, Twitter, Google +
Sunday, March 15, 2015	Promote CSI Faculty and Staff Author talk series (CLUE credit event)	students & faculty	Facebook, Twitter, Google +
Tuesday, March 17, 2015	Promote new books (with photos)	students & faculty	Instagram (syndicates on Facebook)
Thursday, March 19, 2015	Promote photos of spring-like weather on Instagram	students	Instagram (syndicates on Facebook)
Saturday, March 21, 2015	Promote film screening on April 21, 2015 with Facebook event and film poster (CLUE credit)	students & faculty	Facebook, Twitter, Google +

Sample Social Media Promotional Schedule February 1–March 21, 2015 spreadsheet by Mark Aaron Polger, First-Year Experience Librarian, College of Staten Island, CUNY. Used with permission.

No matter what columns you add to your calendar, how it's formatted, or how far ahead you plan—it's critical that your library have just *one* editorial calendar for its content. Don't split it up into separate calendars for each department or each content type, for example. It's important that the entire team can see the full pattern of content creation, and having just one editorial calendar makes planning content more effective and less likely to be redundant.

BOTTOM LINE: Even a basic editorial calendar can save your library time and from the ongoing pressure of knowing what and when to post. It also allows you to more clearly tie content to goals and audiences.

Getting the Most out of Your Content

You already know that content marketing, and even planning content marketing, is a lot of work. (More than you might have bargained for!) It's more work, and we're all struggling to have our content noticed in a world where more content is being constantly created by nearly everyone and everything around us. The very act of creating content takes more thought and effort than it might have before this era of overwhelming content quantity. Don't let your content go to waste after just one go-round. Good marketers repurpose their content in many ways. Essentially, the best practice is to get the most "bang for your buck" out of what you've spent so much time creating.

However, note that re-purposing content is not re-posting content. First, one piece of content is often transformed into one or more other types. For example, a long-form blog post could potentially be used to create a series of tweets. It could also, possibly, be transformed into an infographic. Maybe there are images that could be posted to Instagram or Pinterest. Perhaps there are several images that could be used to create an Animoto animated slideshow.

Second, re-purposed content needs to be correctly formatted for the platform on which it will be posted. Dr. Susanna Gebauer, of the

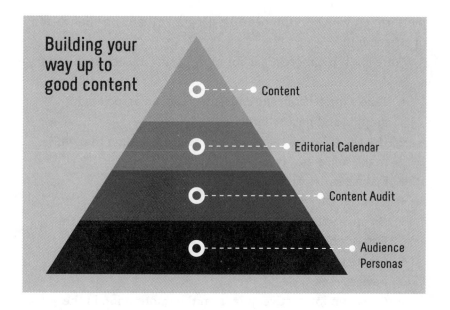

marketing company The Social Marketers, writes: "While repurposing content should be part of any content marketing strategy, each network has its own manners and tolerated behavior. Each network also has its own ideal post formats and text limits. What is easily acceptable in one network might simply be spam in another. If I can see at first glance, that the post originated somewhere else and was automatically spammed to another place, I will definitely not engage in any way or share your post. If you tweet, I will not respond to your tweet on Facebook—why should I?"[8]

Gebauer's point is one that is, unfortunately, ignored by too many libraries. Often, I will see libraries' tweets that simply contain links to content elsewhere. If your library tweets a link to some content on Pinterest, that won't even show up as an image. It will be ignored by everyone. Remember content shock: It's all too easy for people to ignore your content already. If your content isn't optimized for the platform on which it is appearing, it's got virtually no chance at all of succeeding.

Here are some more ideas for repurposing a piece of content:

+ Take a quote from the content, create an associated graphic and post to Pinterest
+ Use the title as a tweet, or compose a variation that will make sense as a tweet
+ Make a series of "handy tips" videos
+ Create a FAQ board on Pinterest
+ Create a slide deck and post to SlideShare and/or to the library's blog or website
+ Create a list of useful, older content that readers might have missed
+ Create an interactive quiz from the information in the content

By the way, the content audit is yet another source for planning re-purposed content. Take a look at your library's older stuff, and see what possibilities might exist for reusing it. Plug those into your editorial calendar when you're running a little low on ideas, or when those older topics might coincide with an upcoming program or holiday.

BOTTOM LINE: Professional marketers plan more than one use for nearly everything they create. Re-purposing content is a strategy that makes the most efficient use out of the content you have.

Getting More Ideas

As I mentioned earlier, it's all too easy to look at the upcoming events calendar at your library and just plan to promote those chronologically, via content. Certainly, you'll want to do this with some high priority events, but not every event at your library is worthy of content creation, when you're competing in already overcrowded arena. Your content needs variety to catch people's attention. You have to prioritize: a high percentage of promotional content is going to turn people away.

This begs the question: Where else can we get ideas for content? The content audit may provide some older material that can be repurposed, but that likely won't be enough in perpetuity.

Remember that libraries are chock-full of content! Interesting information discovered in books or tidbits about favorite authors is always available. Your staff and/or faculty is also a source of content—highlighting them, and their unique talents and interests, also provides some behind-the-scenes interest in your library.

Beyond that, some other ideas, to get ideas:

+ Professional development events: Did you bring back interesting ideas? Use those to get feedback about possibly implementing them at the library. This also gives people outside of the library a deeper look at what libraries do.
+ Is there a productivity tool or app you can't live without? Share it.
+ Look for interesting stories about libraries, reading, or studying, or stories that are related to your specific community. Share those.
+ Share little-known tips or tutorials for using specific resources.

+ Find memorable quotes. (Bonus points if they're funny or entertaining.)
+ Contests where users can easily create content can be effective, as long as very little effort is involved. Funny caption contests are often a draw for engagement, and prizes don't have to be big.
+ Use commonly asked reference questions as starting points. If your library gets a lot of requests concerning new car reviews, create a quick guide to getting started to buying a new car. Something like this can be especially effective as an infographic.
+ When new books arrive, do an "unboxing" video as a way to preview what's new at the library.
+ Do a Google Hangout or Twitter chat with a staff member on a particular topic that has appeal to at least one of your library's core audiences.

Don't forget to be flexible and, as Jessica Gioglio, the director of the Content Lab at Sprinklr and co-author of *The Power of Visual Storytelling* says, to "provide value at the point of need."[9] An example of libraries already doing this can be seen when a famous author passes away. Many libraries will post a list of the author's works, connected to their online catalogs, so that people can easily reserve their favorites. Other libraries will do something similar when there is a national or local tragedy; post a list of resources for dealing with the situation, or perhaps historical context for the event. Always be on the lookout for ways for your library to provide help or resources; this can make for timely and valuable content.

Lastly, you should be aware of a tool used by professionals. Buzzsumo (www.buzzsumo.com/) is a research and monitoring tool with functionality that is of use to library content marketers. One of Buzzumo's main functions that can help you get content ideas is its ability to search on keywords and get results that show what is the most often shared content on the Web.

While Buzzsumo does not, as of this writing, have a freemium model, you can still benefit tremendously from this free keyword search tool as follows:

+ Brainstorm ideas from popular content
+ Get an idea of how successful your chosen topic might be, based on existing metrics
+ You can find other, relevant content to share with your own audiences

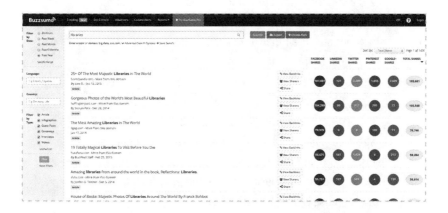

Words of Wisdom from the Field
Writing a Strategy Guide

Angela Hursh is the Content Team Leader in the Marketing Department at the Public Library of Cincinnati and Hamilton County in Cincinnati, Ohio. She is the author of two blogs: Content Marketing for Libraries and Bite from the Past. In her past life, she was an Emmy award-winning journalist. She lives with her videographer husband, two daughters, and enjoys reading and cooking from vintage cookbooks.

There's a critical piece missing in today's library marketing world which can be encompassed in one phrase—content strategy. Many of our colleagues at great libraries across the country are struggling to connect with current and prospective cardholders because they create and distribute promotional messages without a content strategy. Random promotions for programs, book clubs, and story times aren't resonating with their audience, and libraries are wondering why circulation and attendance is dropping. They lack a clear and decisive marketing direction and without one, their institution is in jeopardy.

Most brands would kill for the kind of customer loyalty we enjoy. Everyone loves their library. So why are libraries struggling with growth? Our audience has grown more sophisticated. They're savvy about marketing, and they can see a promotional pitch a mile away. It turns them off. The brands thriving in this new market have figured out how to make a connection with their customers through a clear and concise content strategy.

Library marketing must inspire cardholders enough to drive them to action, and that's incredibly difficult. It's not enough anymore to tout the vague concept of "library is good for everyone." You've got to make your community see why their library is an indispensable part of their everyday lives. That's a difficult concept to communicate. Without a clear-cut content strategy, you're just throwing spaghetti at the wall and most of it isn't sticking.

Content strategy must be the driving force of everything you do. It is the wheel of your ship. It will help you define a niche audience for whom you will market. When you drill down and focus on a target audience, your message is more likely to resonate and inspire action. A strategy also gives you permission to say "no" when you're asked to market anything that doesn't support your objectives. You won't be wasting energy creating content that won't drive results.

To create your content strategy, focus on these key elements:

1. What is my library's mission statement and what are its core values? Your marketing is a foundational pillar for your library's success. Everything you do should support the growth of your system. Everything you create—blogs, podcasts, newsletters, e-mails, graphics, and more—must support your mission statement and core values.

2. How can I target my messages for maximum results? The biggest mistake library marketers make is trying to be all things to all people. Successful brands focus their content strategy on niche audiences. Targeted audiences help you fine-tune your message. They feel more personal to the receiver and that makes them more effective.

3. Keep your message focused on your customer, not on you. Constantly ask yourself: What does my cardholder want and need? What keeps them up at night? Your content strategy should include a desire to help relieve those pain points.

4. Define what success will look like. Tracking the effectiveness of every piece of content you produce will help you determine what works and adjust your messages. Decide at the outset what metrics you will use to gauge success. Then keep tabs religiously.

5. Don't be afraid to experiment. Your content marketing strategy should include room for "errors of enthusiasm"—great ideas that don't exactly work right off the bat but that lead you to something really inspiring.

Above all, make sure authenticity is a key part of your strategy. Be committed to speaking conversationally and on the same level as your cardholders. People like to be made to feel smart, valued, and appreciated. Don't talk over your cardholders' heads. Engage them on their level. Listen to them. And then provide them with the means to improve their lives. They'll be left with the feeling that their library is more than a home for great books . . . it's a great resource they must have in order to survive and be successful.

BOTTOM LINE: Coming up with content ideas can sometimes seem like sitting down in front of a blank piece of paper. Use the resources and tools available to help fill in any blanks on your library's editorial calendar.

NOTES

1. Lisa Toner, "How Does Your Content Marketing Compare? [NEW DATA],"May 26, 2015, www.socialbro.com/blog/how-does-your-content-marketing-compare-new-data.
2. Angela Watercutter, "How Oreo Won the Marketing Super Bowl With a Timely Blackout Ad on Twitter," February 4, 2013, www.wired.com/2013/02/oreo-twitter-super-bowl/.
3. Angela Hursh, "The Biggest Library Marketing Obstacles and How to Overcome Them," https://librarycontentmarketing.wordpress.com/2015/02/11/the-five-biggest-library-marketing-obstacles-and-how-to-overcome-them-with-content-marketing/.
4. Content Marketing Institute, "Content Marketing Framework: Plan," http://contentmarketinginstitute.com/plan/.
5. Anthony Gaenzle, "Why You Need to Conduct a Full Audit for Successful Content Marketing, March 14, 2014, http://contentmarketinginstitute.com/2014/03/conduct-full-audit-successful-content-marketing/."
6. Single Grain, "The Step-by-Step Guide to Conducting a Content Audit," http://singlegrain.com/the-step-by-step-guide-to-conducting-a-content-audit/.
7. Nathan Ellering, "10 Reasons Your Editorial Calendar Sucks (and How to Make It the Best)," www.convinceandconvert.com/content-marketing/improve-editorial-calendar/.
8. Susanna Gebauer, "Repurposing Content or Cross-Posting—Efficiency vs. Spam," December 1, 2014, http://blog.thesocialms.com/repurposing-content-cross-posting-efficiency-vs-spam/#XHTW000cZEu516yD.99.
9. Jessica Gioglio, "3 Tactics to Surprise and Delight Your Fans," www.convinceandconvert.com/social-media-case-studies/surprise-and-delight/.

Writing So People Might Give a Damn

"When something can be read without effort,
great effort has gone into its writing."

—Enrique Jardiel Poncela

It should come as no surprise to anyone that writing for an online audience is different than how many of us were taught to write in school. The Web is a very different medium than traditional print. Most online readers are likely to be task-oriented in their approach, or they will scan for relevant keywords that attract their attention. In a research study of online reading behavior, usability expert Jakob Nielsen found that "on the average webpage, users have time to read at most 28% of the words during an average visit; 20% is more likely."[1]

Think about how you, yourself, probably use the Web. You probably only rarely read a post or article in its entirety. Generally speaking, online readers spend little time with specific pieces of content. They are often looking to accomplish a specific goal, or for phrases that clearly demonstrate Jay Baer's "Youtility" concept; they have an obvious benefit.

These behaviors make getting attention for content more difficult, but now add them to the idea of "content shock." It's a double whammy: potential readers spend less time on content, and then there is, overall, much more content available. This can present a dismal picture for the content creator. At the very least, it's going to be a challenge to entice people to consume *your* content.

In order to be competitive in this arena, you're going to have to recognize that you'll need to start by strengthening the foundation of your content: the writing. User-friendly writing prevents readers from abandoning your content immediately. If the content is poorly written or badly organized, readers will go elsewhere to find something more appealing. There is simply too much out there already, competing for users' attention, for you to knowingly construct anything inferior.

Start with the Headline

Whether you call it a "post title," a "heading," or something else, the headline of your content is the single most critical contact point with potential readers. Not only is it the first thing readers see, it is the part that will likely determine if a possible reader will go further into the content or even engage with it. While 80 percent of people read a headline, only 20 percent of the audience actually will click it.[2] If a reader has made it to your specific content in the overwhelming sea of what's available, your headline is often the turning point: it is usually a determining factor as to whether or not the content is successful.

There are several factors that can make or break a headline:

+ **Length.** There is some debate among professionals about how long a headline should be. Some advocate for short and sweet, while others prefer a more verbose headline. However, one criterion to consider is how the headline will appear in search results. According to marketing consultancy Quick Sprout, the maximum character count, before the headline is cut off in search results, is 65.[3] Quick Sprout also says that people only read the first three and the last three words of a given headline. Since making your content findable should be a concern, these statistics seems to favor shorter headlines.

+ **Inform and hook.** This is actually much like print journalism: the headline should clearly state what the content is about, and not attempt to be clever or "cutesy." Online content headlines do differ from print headlines, however, in that they should not attempt to simply summarize the content. This practice can often result in very bland headlines. For example: "Research Databases for Your Next Term Paper," versus something like "Jump Start Your Next Term Paper with These." The latter not only has an implied benefit, but leaves the exact nature of the content vague, choosing instead to focus on the payoff and invite readers to read further. It also can be tempting to infuse headlines with clever puns, or abstract concepts not known to readers. Erik Dekers, owner of Professional Blog Service and author of several books about social media, writes: "Don't use your headline as some secret code for the reader. Don't make it a final punchline where people flip on the "a-ha" lightbulb when they reach the end. Write a headline that immediately tells the reader what the piece is about, so they can decide whether to read it."[4]

+ **Promise.** Good headlines have a promise that they make to the reader. This is the payoff they will get, if they continue to read. This factor should heavily incorporate the personas you have created for your library's content marketing. You should already have a good idea of what the pain points and needs of your audience are. If your headline is not making a promise that your content will fulfill, or explaining a need it will help with, start over. Remember, though, that your content *will* have to live up to the promise made in the headline. Don't allow your headline to lie. If you are promising readers "10 Amazing Ways a Librarian Can Help," that's exactly what your readers should get.

+ **Language.** Language is another area where your content marketing personas will come into play. Knowing what kinds of words your audience will understand, or respond to, can make your headline more effective. Keep in mind that readers are scanning your titles for words that are relevant to them. What's going to resonate? "Finals Week" versus "End of the semester?" "Book club" versus "book discussion group?" Using the terms your audience prefers will help your skimming readers grasp the possibilities of your content more quickly.

A headline strategy that Neil Patel of Quick Sprout advocates is an overall formula of Number or Trigger Word + Adjective + Keyword + Promise. Here's how that might work:

Original headline:
"New Books at the Library for July"

Headline with Quick Sprout formula:
"Ten New Books Perfect for Your Trip to the Beach"

Why is the re-made headline better? The formula addresses many of the criteria that make for a good headline. The headline itself, in the revised version, makes a promise about perfect beach reads, using the word "new" as the attracting adjective. Content that features a set number of items (often referred to as "list posts," or even "listicles") are very popular online. The keywords, in this case, are "book," "trip" and "beach." Any of the three may catch a reader's eye, depending on their interests. In the original version, it's unlikely that "library" will be a relevant keyword to readers; keywords need to show a purpose aligned with the person reading. People scan for what applies to *them*. It's more likely that the three keywords in the second version will apply directly to a reader's self-interest. The use of the word "your" in the second headline also shows who the benefit of the content is for. Never forget, when writing a headline, that it must strongly appeal to the intended audience and is not meant to directly promote the library.

BOTTOM LINE: Headlines matter, and are often the point at which you gain or lose readers. Spend time on your headline, and focus on making it resonate with your audience.

Take a Critical Look at the Content

Once you've succeeded in getting the reader's interest with the headline, it does no good to lose them once they get to the content. Whether you wrote the headline before or after you created the main material, you're going to need to exert some effort to optimize your content.

Voice. If you're accustomed to writing in the passive voice, you're going to need to change your habits. The active voice is essential to clear online communication. Consider this example:

"Your research can benefit from the assistance of a librarian."
Versus
"Our librarians will help you get your research done."

Active voice emphasizes the person or people doing the action, and also decreases the likelihood of your language sounding bureaucratic.

Tone. The kind of language you use is important. A guide from New York University wisely notes: "Online readers expect a personal, upbeat tone in web writing. They find bureaucratic writing so offensive and out-of-place that they simply ignore the message it's trying to convey. To avoid bureaucratic language, turn the tone down a notch. Search out and destroy jargon."[5] Most experts will tell you that you need to write like you talk. The demeanor of your post should be conversational. The method for writing a press release and the method of writing an online post are not the same and need different approaches. The expectations of the two formats by their readers are complete opposites: a press agent reading a release expects a more formal tone, while casual readers online want a much more relaxed piece.

Frontload. Journalists use the practice of frontloading stories to make their articles more useful to the reader. This means that the information that is most important to the audience goes into the first paragraph, and supporting details come after. The idea is that you need to prove the value of the content first; readers will go on to read the rest if the value of the post is definite. Many people are used to building to a conclusion, so this may be a significant change in approach. Since readers scan content, however, this is much more effective. Your audience may never make it to the end of the content, meaning that they would otherwise not make it to the conclusion.

Tell stories. People not only enjoy stories, they also find that stories make your content much more relatable. Stories give your content an emotional component that enables readers to connect on a more human level. Chris Brogan, CEO of the Owner Media Group, suggests starting with the reader as the hero of the story.[6] For example, tell a story where a patron was successful using the library's services, but don't even mention the library until near the end. This is keeping in line with the concept of being useful, not promotional. Don't be afraid to use stories from patrons (with permission, of course), or use stories about yourself. One of the most popular posts on my own blog demonstrates this concept. I told a story about how I inadvertently lost my credit card in a soda vending machine. My expectations from using other credit card-enabled vending machines didn't match the user interface on this particular machine, and so I ended up with a very bad user experience. I used this story to help people understand how a library website's design can cause negative experiences as well, if the design deviates from expected norms. The fact that it was a personal story kept the reader's attention and helped them to relate to my point.

Feature the experience. If your content is telling patrons about something newly available, it's more likely to resonate if it emphasizes the experience they will have by taking advantage of it. Too often, libraries focus on just the feature or benefit, without delving any deeper. Take this example: A library gets a new research database. Next, consider the following approaches:

Feature: The library has a new database.
Benefit: You'll get higher-quality information with the new database.
Experience: Blow away your teachers or professors. Credible, professional sources add information to your research not available via Google and make you look like a more committed student.

Go beyond just the bare-bones benefit, and tie content to what result the patron might feel or experience.

Think about sharing. You may have created interesting content, but it does much more good if it is also shared by others. There is a lot of advice out there for helping content to be shared, but here is some of the most important:

Lean consistently towards the positive. Content with a positive sentiment tends not only to go viral more often,[7] but also is more likely to match the kinds of content readers are looking for. Pew Research found that 35 percent of men and 43 percent of women are on Facebook primarily to see funny or entertaining content.[8] Not everything you write is probably going to be positive (if the parking lot is closed for repaving, for example), but strive to make the negative posts humorous or interesting. ("5 Ways Librarians Kill Time While Waiting for the Parking Lot to Dry.")

Longer is better. It might seem odd, especially when one considers that tweets max out at 140 characters and Vine videos at only six seconds, but longer posts are actually more likely to be shared.[9] The additional advantage to longer content is that it can also be more easily broken up or transformed into other content types, making re-purposing efforts less painful.

Make it visual. It's no secret that online content usually is more effective with a visual component, such as a photo or video. Tweets with an image are more likely to be retweeted[10] Socialbakers.com found that posts with photos saw the most engagement—accounting for a whopping 87 percent of total interactions with Facebook brand pages.[11] The Web has become increasingly visual in nature; all one has to do is consider the meteoric rise of newer services such as Pinterest, Instagram, and Snapchat over the past couple of years. Help your content stand out among the masses with a unique visual piece.

BOTTOM LINE: Online content needs to be optimized to be at its best. Use these practices to make sure that what you create has a fighting chance against the competition.

Make it Palatable

Just when you *think* you've optimized your content, there's yet more work to be done. How your content is presented is at least as important as what it contains (and some might argue, even more important). Your content has to make a first impression: if it looks like paragraphs of verbosity, it won't succeed in the competitive environment of the Web. Nobody's got time to wade through tons of text, and they won't. People will simply go elsewhere, no matter what your headline promises.

One of the most meaningful changes you can make is to insure that your content is scannable. Recognize that how people see online content is much like a newspaper: people don't generally read from top to bottom. They're looking for words that are immediately of interest. You can help them with that scanning by doing the following:

+ **Chunking.** While paragraphs do break apart content, they're not enough on their own. Make good use of subheadings and subsections, to make it easier for readers to get to what they're interested in. Often, chunks also help with re-purposing of content later on.

+ **Going short.** While long-form content is more likely to be shared, the actual sentences and paragraph in that content need to be short. Usability.gov says: "The ideal standard is no more than 20 words per sentence, five sentences per paragraph. Use dashes instead of semi-colons or, better yet, break the sentence into two. It is ok to start a sentence with 'and,' 'but,' or 'or' if it makes things clear and brief."[12] Going shorter may require you to break some grammar rules, but that's not an issue: a casual tone is essential.

+ **Make bulleted and numbered lists your friends.** You'll notice that this book makes heavy use of these tactics, and for good reason. They force chunking, and also draw attention to individual points. Sean D'Souza, writing for Copyblogger .com, compares bullets to flashing Christmas lights. "They flash because of their ability to create curiosity. And not just a little bit of curiosity, but a massive amount of curiosity."[13] They also make content less intimidating than a page of just straight text might.

+ ***Don't be afraid of italic and bold.*** These formatting styles also help to draw attention and to distinguish unique chunks of content from one another. Specially formatted items are visual cues for your readers. (Underlining should never be used, as it is the standard convention for distinguishing hyperlinks from plain text.)

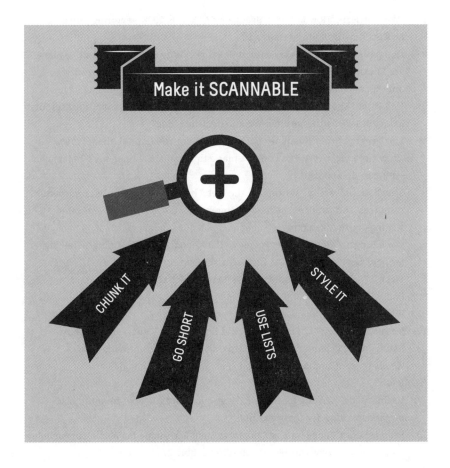

BOTTOM LINE: How content is formatted is just as crucial as the content itself. Get used to breaking down your content into smaller sections so readers can quickly scan for pieces relevant to them.

NOTES

1. Jakob Nielsen, "How Little Do Users Read?," May 6, 2008, www.nngroup.com/articles/how-little-do-users-read/.
2. Douglas Karr, "What Makes a Good Headline?: Why Only 20% of Your Readers are Clicking Through on Your Article Title," August 19, 2014, https://www.marketingtechblog.com/write-incredible-titles-headlines/.
3. Neil Patel, "The Formula for a Perfect Headline," July 3, 2014, www.quicksprout.com/2014/07/03/the-formula-for-a-perfect-headline/.
4. Eric Deckers, "Your Headlines Suck. Here's What You Can Do About It," www.convinceandconvert.com/content-marketing/your-headlines-suck-heres-what-you-can-do-about-it/.
5. New York University, "Writing for the Web," https://www.nyu.edu/employees/resources-and-services/media-and-communications/styleguide/website/writing-for-the-web.html.
6. Chris Brogan, "How Do I Get People to Care About What I'm Doing?—Tell Bigger Stories," September 24, 2012, http://chrisbrogan.com/theflag.
7. Mark W. Schaefer, The Content Code (Mark W. Schaefer, 2015).
8. Ibid.
9. Ibid.
10. Jesse Mawhinney, "17 Stats You Should Know About Visual Content Marketing in 2015," January 22, 2015, http://blog.hubspot.com/marketing/visual-content-marketing-strategy.
11. Ibid.
12. Usability.gov, "Writing for the Web," www.usability.gov/how-to-and-tools/methods/writing-for-the-web.html.
13. Sean D'Souza, "The Flashing Christmas Light Technique for Writing Irresistible Bullet Points," www.copyblogger.com/irresistible-bullet-points/.

Common Mistakes
Getting Better, Going Forward

"I always say the minute I stop making mistakes is the minute I stop learning and I've definitely learned a lot."

—Miley Cyrus

Whether we're new to content marketing, or have been doing it for years, content marketing is still a process with a learning curve. Everyone makes mistakes as they learn what works best for their libraries. You are unlikely to succeed right away, and that's OK. Realizing that success may be a long-term venture prevents constant disappointment. However, you can advance your progress, at least a little bit, by considering advice from seasoned professionals, and the stories of library colleagues who have already had useful experiences. Start with making sure you're not falling into some of these common traps, listed below.

Mistake #1: Shouting as Loud as We Can

"Content marketing is sold wrong. We're told to shout as loud as we can . . . and an anxious audience will be anxiously awaiting our every word."[1] These words are from Ryan Hanley, the author of *Content Warfare: How to Find Your Audience, Tell Your Story and Win the Battle for Attention Online.* His point is well taken: too many libraries make the mistake of simply blogging or posting without an actual plan that might lead to real results. Granted, it *is* easier to simply create content, sit back and hope something happens. It may seem like this book has been full of "have a plan or else!" But, hopefully, you've learned by now that the easy way isn't the effective way.

If nothing else, a library needs to account for economics. Content marketing isn't free. Staff time, at the very least, costs money. If the staff person writing a blog post takes two hours to write a blog post, and makes $30.00 an hour, what happens if that blog post gets zero engagement or is never shared? There's no progress towards the library's content marketing goals, and that's $60.00 the library just wasted. Imagine that same scenario happening on a weekly or even daily basis. What library can afford this kind of inefficacy? It's time to stop shouting and to go forward with a strategy.

Mistake #2: Ignoring Staff Experience

Let's assume that you, the reader, are the content marketer (or perhaps lucky enough to be part of a marketing team) for your library. How many other people work in your institution? Probably several; perhaps even many. Take a moment to consider how their daily interactions with patrons differ from yours. Unless you also work on the front lines with the public, it's likely that their experiences and viewpoints are very different from your own.

Remember: content marketing is essentially telling stories. Stories humanize organizations. Your library's staff is a cornucopia of untapped content potential. Spend some time talking to your staff about some of what they experience out on the floor or at a desk. They've got stories, guaranteed! Of course, some won't be fit to share publicly, but ask them to tell you about the most rewarding transaction they've had in the past week or two. Ask them if they've made any mistakes that were humorous, in retrospect. What's the funniest thing they've heard a child say in story time? Look to your staff for stories about staff celebrations, or benign pranks. Collect their best research tips, their most unique hobbies, their favorite books. Not only will these kinds of stories humanize your library, but they help patrons get to know the people inside of it. Staff stories can be an endless source of content inspiration.

Mistake #3: Creating, Then Forgetting the Next Step

Let's not pretend that coming up with content is always easy. It's a lot of work. It can be such a relief to push that newest post or graphic out to the world, that we can forget that the job isn't yet finished. Not promoting content is part of that "shouting as loud as we can" mentality: we can easily fall into the habit of thinking that people will know about the content, just because it is now created. "If a piece of content was created and placed online but no one saw it, does it really exist?"[2] asks Chris Bird, writing for The Business Journals. The realistic answer might be "no."

You already know, from prior chapters, that the competition is way too stiff to simply lean back and say "Done!" There are many ways promote your content, even beyond regular social media. Don't forget e-mail newsletters, paid ads on Google or Facebook, even offline posters. You might even ask a local business or organization to mention it, if the content is something you think their patrons might also find useful. Recognize that creating your valuable content is just that: valuable. Don't squander it by not promoting it.

Mistake #4: Not Making It Shareable

You've created this great content: now, you need to make it easy for people to spread it around. Mark W. Schaefer, author of *The Content Code*, says "Business results on the web don't come from content; they come from content that moves."[3] Engagement is absolutely wonderful, but we have to plan for our content to do more than just engage. Consider the following, to increase your content's chances of moving:

+ **Have sharing buttons.** If you're posting to, say, Facebook or Twitter, sharing mechanisms are built in and you don't need to worry about this. But what about your library's website or blog? If you don't make it simple for readers to share, they almost certainly won't. There are many plugins for most content management systems (e.g. WordPress, Drupal) that can do this, or other kinds of add-ons such as Filament's Flare plugin (http://filament.io/flare) or ShareThis (www.sharethis.com). Don't give your readers a ready excuse not to share the content.

+ **Certain kinds of content move more than others.** Posts that are lists (often referred to as "listicles") and posts that explain "why" about something are shared the most often.[4] List posts are often very scannable, and "why" posts clearly provide information the reader may have been searching for or find immediately useful. Not all of your content will (or necessarily should) be in these formats, but use them at least occasionally and measure how they do against other types.

+ *People share that which makes them look good.* Mark W. Schaeffer, spends a whole chapter on shareability in his book *The Content Code.* He points out that sharing is a very psychological, emotional act. By sharing, and identifying with, your content, a reader is making a statement about him/herself. "Sharing an idea from this book makes a statement about you, just like your choice in jeans, car or a soft drink. It says, I concur. I am aligned. I think this author is smart and I am smart; therefore I will share it. This book is cool and I am cool, so I will share it."[5] Give this concept some thought, because it goes beyond just making sure there is a payoff in your content. If you are providing a new service, it might be easy to point out the direct benefits to the reader. Will those benefits be easy to see if they share?

Mistake #5: Not Making All of This a Habit

In some ways, this is the pot calling the kettle black—this is a mistake that I, personally, struggle with on a regular basis. For example: even though I use an editorial calendar for my own organization, I still sometimes forget to allow the time to plan ahead. It's all too easy to get excited for a while . . . and then, that excitement wanes.

Content marketing, is a process that only really pays off over the long term. Which means, slow and steady wins the race. The "steady" part can be hard. A dead stop after a lot of momentum, however, harms your efforts. You have to make a commitment. Get your system(s) in place to make sure this happens. Make sure you have administrative buy-in for spending the time on this. It comes down to having the supports in place to make sure you can give this consistent effort.

Words of Wisdom from the Field
Common Mistakes of Content Marketing

Kathy Dempsey is a consultant and trainer through her business, Libraries Are Essential, and is the author of *The Accidental Library Marketer* (Information Today, Inc., 2009). Her work is dedicated to helping librarians and information professionals promote their value and expertise in order to gain respect and funding. Kathy has been the Editor of the Marketing Library Services newsletter for 21 years and was formerly Editor-in-Chief of *Computers in Libraries* magazine. She also blogs at The 'M' Word, and is an active member of the New Jersey Library Association.

If you define "content marketing" as telling the stories about your library's services, collections, events, or successes, you'll have plenty to promote. But beware these common marketing mistakes:

+ **WRITING EVERYTHING LIKE IT'S A PRESS RELEASE.** There's a big difference between a press release and an interesting story. The hard-news style of a press release is full of facts but devoid of feeling. People enjoy and remember stories because they elicit feelings. Use each writing style at the appropriate times.

+ **TELLING STORIES IN THE THIRD PERSON OR MAKING ACTIONS ANONYMOUS.** Phrases such as "This was done successfully" don't give credit where it's due. Great stories have real characters. Use the names of librarians; identify them as helpful experts. Create a "voice" that allows people to think of the library as a friend, not as a cold, bricks-and-mortar entity. Look at the difference in these one-line stories: "The patron filled out an online job application in the library, and he got an interview 2 weeks later." "Sally, our business librarian, spent time helping Jim complete an online job application, and he got an interview 2 weeks later."

+ **FORGETTING THAT "CONTENT" IS ALL AROUND YOU.** If you're having trouble thinking of "content to post," then you're going about it the wrong way. Library stories aren't things you make up; they're things you observe. Get out of your office and look at the activities inside and outside of the building. You're surrounded by real, human stories!

+ **NOT GATHERING AND USING QUOTES AND STORIES FROM REAL PEOPLE.** You, as a library employee, shouldn't be telling all of the library's stories in your own voice. Instead, use the words and feelings of people who use your services and attend your events. You can gather quotes by chatting with people, by passing out post-event surveys, by asking for quotes or stories on a bulletin board or website; or you can take them from existing collections. Just look at the powerful testimonials that these projects gathered:

My Library Story: http://mystory.gale.com
Libraries Changed My Life: http://librarieschangedmylife.tumblr.com
Living Stories, Living Libraries: http://living-stories-living-libraries.tumblr.com

+ **USING THE "ONE SIZE FITS ALL" PLAN.** You wouldn't tell the same story to a group of preschoolers as you would to a group of teens or a group of businesspeople. It's vital to target different messages to different audiences. And usually, different folks follow different media. So don't automatically post the same message on Facebook, Pinterest, Twitter, and your blog. Study your followers; understand where various target audiences are; share info accordingly. You may even need to have separate accounts for separate audiences. And remember to use the right language and keywords for each group you're trying to reach.

+ **SKIPPING THE EVALUATIONS AND ANALYSES.** If you continue to do the same thing all the time without ever measuring results or checking statistics, you may keep making the same mistakes forever. Trying, failing, tweaking, and trying again puts you on the road to success. But trying and just hoping you hit the mark doesn't ever help you improve.

+ **WORKING WITHOUT A CONTENT MARKETING PLAN.** A content marketing plan doesn't have to be elaborate, and you don't need to hire a consultant to write it. Something as simple as this can serve as a plan: "Post 4x/week: 1 joke/cartoon, 1 patron quote, 1 event announcement, 1 engagement question." Of course, it's useful to have more goals and details. But as long as there's a plan that aligns with your library's mission, and it's written down and approved (to ensure that you stick to it), then even the most basic plan can help you stay on schedule and on message.

BOTTOM LINE: Creating the content is a process that involves a lot of work and thought. Involve library staff, make it shareable and don't forget to actually promote it.

Visual Content: A Picture Says a Lot of Words

It's no secret that the Web has become increasingly visual: images not only garner more attention, but they've been proven to increase effectiveness of associated content. Pictures are powerful, and can easily help tell your library's story. Text paired with photographs or video is easier to process and usually more interesting than words alone. A survey by MDG Advertising showed that content with an eye-catching image received 94 percent more total views than content without an image.[6] Not every piece of content you create necessarily has to have some kind of visual but, when do you use one, be sure to consider the following criteria:

+ **Quality counts.** There are now many tools to help you create images and infographics. If you're not a digital artist, they can help tremendously. However, if you don't have an artistic eye yourself, make sure you get support from someone who does. The competition for attention is tough, but you don't want to attract the wrong kind of attention. Whatever you create needs to look professional. Kathi Kruse, of the agency Kruse Control, Inc., says: "There are great tools like Canva and PicMonkey but let's face it, if you can't tell the difference between good and poor quality visual content, these tools will not help you."[7]

+ **Optimize your images.** That image that looks great in Photoshop may not look quite so terrific once it's posted to a social network. Test your images by creating a post on your chosen social media, but don't publish. This allows you to preview it first. Some images can look distorted, or are zoomed in too close or too far away to make out the details. Most social networks have stated preferred images sizes and/or ratios. This is just a matter of simple googling; for example, try "cheat sheet for Facebook images." (Parameters may change periodically, so you may wish to add the current date to your search, to make sure you're not getting old information.)

+ **Beware of text.** The point of a visual is to be visual . . . so, don't cover it up with a lot of text. Too much text makes the image harder to cognitively digest. Text may also be cut off, such as in the case of a Twitter feed, where the whole image is rarely shown in-stream. Let your image do the talking.

+ **Brand your images.** Remember that images not only need to look professional, they need to look like they were from your library. Brand your images: use your library's logo, name, and website URL. Ideally, you don't want your visuals to appear as being totally random. It's not always possible to make your images appear similar, but you do want people to consistently know where they came from.

BOTTOM LINE: Visuals are an important addition to most content. Don't let them appear like they were done by a nonprofessional or didn't come from your library.

Some Stories from the Field

There are a lot of staff, just like us, struggling with content shock and learning some of the rudiments of content marketing. Some would like to share their experiences, so that you can benefit from them. Here are a few:

+ Sometimes, challenges are less conceptual and more of the practical nature. Library marketing staff may have worked for months on materials, only to have pertinent information change shortly after printing or publication. Monica Ruane Rogers, assistant professor and research and instruction librarian at Manderino Library (California University of Pennsylvania), related that her staff created giveaways with her library's AIM chat name on it, but shortly thereafter the library began using LibGuides and stopped using the AIM chat service. At one point even the university's URL changed, invalidating a good number of promotional materials. She since recommends being prepared with creative solutions (they used stickers over the old information, to redirect people to the correct sources) and try to keep editable copies of materials in-house, so that changes can be made more easily.

+ One common issue is paring down information to what's actually essential. It's not always immediately obvious what is marketing, and what is information. One academic librarian pointed to an information handout about library services and resources. It gave so much in one flyer, that it was completely overwhelming to students. The university library, as a result, is currently redesigning it to be more user-friendly.

+ Mark Aaron Polger, assistant professor and first-year experience librarian at the College of Staten Island, City University of New York, shared that he struggles with engagement with posts on social media. His library can see that people do view the posts, and will often "like" them, but rarely comment or share. He is working to change the verbiage for his posts to better accommodate each platform.

BOTTOM LINE: You are not alone! Library marketers everywhere are striving to understand new methods and new patron behaviors, to better get the stories of their libraries in front of their audiences.

NOTES

1. Ryan Hanley, "7 Ways to Fail at Content Marketing," November 4, 2014, www.ryanhanley.com/7-ways-to-fail-at-content-marketing/.
2. Chris Bird, "5 reasons why your content marketing fails (and how to prevent it)," August 20, 2015, www.bizjournals.com/bizjournals/how-to/marketing/2015/08/5-reasons-why-content-marketing-fails.html?page=all.
3. Mark W. Schaefer, *The Content Code* (Mark W. Schaefer, 2015).
4. Suzanne Delzio, "Social Sharing Habits: New Research Reveals What People Like to Share," March 24, 2015, www.socialmediaexaminer.com/social-sharing-habits-new-research/.
5. Mark W. Schaefer, *The Content Code* (Mark W. Schaefer, 2015).
6. Rebekah Radice, "How to Create Visual Content Your Audience Will Love," August 3, 2015, http://rebekahradice.com/create-visual-content-your-audience-will-love/.
7. Kathi Kruse, "10 Guaranteed Ways to #Fail at Content Marketing," July 27, 2015, www.krusecontrolinc.com/ways-to-fail-at-content-marketing/.

Are You Actually Succeeding?
(And How Do You Know?)

"You've got to create a great atmosphere of measuring what's right, rather than measuring what you can."

—Robert Rose, Chief Strategy Officer at the Content Marketing Institute

If you've already been tracking any metrics for your content marketing efforts, then you may already have concluded that measuring effectiveness is not an easy job.

Sadly, you'd be right.

As of this writing, there is a great deal of discussion about this topic in the professional content marketer community. There's no shortage of posts, books, and advice about what to measure, and ways to measure it. Virtually all experts agree that effectiveness needs to be calculated, but there's very little agreement beyond that.

To complicate matters, libraries are, at least somewhat, unique. The primary function of libraries typically isn't to sell things, or event to get donations, like many other not-for-profits. Money rarely changes hands at all. This means that the traditional ways in which much marketing is measured don't really apply. Conventionally, content marketing is measured in terms of conversions.

A conversion is when a user takes a specific, desired action. For retail sites, defining a conversion is generally easy. Someone came to their website and then purchased something. Even for other not-for-profits, figuring a conversion is relatively simple. Typically, they want you to donate money or take an advocacy-related action, such as writing your legislator. In both of these instances, there are clear actions that the site owners want visitors to take. The conversion is, essentially, the holy grail of web metrics. It's the thing that really matters. Did the website or post help users take the desired action or not?

For libraries doing content marketing, there's rarely an ultimate, clear act that defines a conversion. Content almost never attempts to direct people to some kind of monetary transaction. The economic value is, at best, murky.

However, this isn't truly new territory for us. Virtually all library administrators are familiar with the difficulty of proving concrete return on investment (ROI) for a library.

Libraries generally provide access to information; historically, that goal has also been difficult to benchmark. Many different statistics are traditionally used to attempt to calculate value: some metrics include physical visitors, circulation counts, program attendees, or website visits. Even with all of those numbers at our disposal, there's still not often an immediate, clear way to say, for example, "One visit to the library equals X dollars in ROI."

It might actually be less of a leap for us, as library staff, to come to the understanding that measuring content marketing is cloudy territory, than it might be for someone coming to this effort from outside of libraries. Perhaps we are more used to the idea that measurement isn't always a clear-cut process, which, as it turns out, is a good thing, since there is still a great deal of debate.

We're not alone in being frustrated. In a report released in 2015 by TrustRadius, 60 percent of the marketers surveyed named "measuring ROI" as their top challenge.[1] This doesn't mean, however, that libraries should give up on figuring out what they get out of content marketing. Rather, it's indicative that we're all in the beginnings of building new foundations for our efforts, and those foundations may not have an exact floor plan. It's a learning curve for marketers, everywhere.

BOTTOM LINE: Measuring content marketing is, at best, an inexact science. Nonetheless, we need to know if what we are doing has effect, and how we can do it better. The need for metrics will always be there, even if the process is in flux.

Things to Think about When You're Getting Started

It's very easy to quickly become overwhelmed with the potential complexity of measuring content marketing work. Take a deep breath, and start by asking these questions:

1. **How will you monitor your channels?** Whether it's various social media accounts, e-mail campaigns, or something else, you'll need to figure out which monitoring tools you'll be using. Built-in channel metrics, such as Facebook Insights? Google Analytics? Specialized software services? Or, some combination of these?

2. **What were the goals, again?** Even though you may imagine the goals you set for your content are only important at the beginning of the planning process, that's not the case. They are also critical for figuring out the ROI of your content. You'll need to work backwards from your goals to define what actually should be measured and evaluated. Goals drive metrics, as well as content decisions.

3. **Which metrics will you use?** As discussed earlier, there's not necessarily a standard set of measurements, even across the marketing industry. Add to this the fact that each channel may have a totally different set of available metrics, making your job sometimes seem like a comparison of apples to oranges. Comparing the numbers of fans/followers on Facebook and Twitter, for example, is not really a fair comparison, since it's generally much easier to gain followers on Twitter than on Facebook. That number also may have little or nothing to do with your overall goals. Michele Linn, vice president of content at the Content Marketing Institute, says: "The metrics that matter most are the ones that are tied to your business goals, so that will vary from company to company. What does management care about the most?"[2] The ones that you choose are commonly referred to as Key Performance Indicators (KPIs). Everyone involved with creating content or reporting on it needs to know what these are, and understand how they impact their content marketing work.

To further focus your thoughts about your library's content marketing reports, ask this powerful question: Would your library spend money to change that number? Content marketing already costs your library money, in staff time if nothing else. Measuring the effects of content marketing is about justifying that time. If an important criterion needs to be changed, will your library want more time and/or money devoted to that?

BOTTOM LINE: Don't dive into measuring stuff without figuring out which metrics best suit your library's particular goals. Make sure that involved staff understand what the KPIs are and use them to drive content creation.

Some Metrics to Measure By

While there is no agreed-upon checklist of what to measure, there are some metrics that are widely recognized as useful for most content marketing campaigns. Not all of these may fit your particular goals, but may be considered as possible benchmarks to start from.

+ **Engagement.** This one applies primarily to social media content. Specific measurements differ from platform to platform: for instance, Facebook has likes, comments and shares, while Twitter has favorites, mentions and retweets. Some forms of engagement, however, have more value than others. A comment on a post is much more active than a simple, passive like. Many people consider actions such as comments and retweets to be the most important, because they generate conversation. However, more experts are coming to believe that the ultimate form of engagement is when someone shares that content with others. Mark W. Schaefer, author of *The Content Code*, refers to this as content that "ignites." The most active form of engagement is when someone believes it is good enough to want to share it.

+ Clickthroughs. Of the people who saw the post, how many clicked a link in it that drove traffic to your website (or, in the case of a library, perhaps the catalog)? Sometimes this also may include downloads of content, such as audio files, ebooks, or documents. Some marketers choose to break out downloads as a separate metric from clickthroughs.

+ Sentiment. Many libraries may be in the enviable position of not having to worry too much about negative reactions to their content. However, it's still good to note any changes in positive versus negative commentary.

+ Audiences. While numbers are great to have, they're not worthwhile without some context. Simply reporting numbers, without any examination, won't help you focus your work. Another question to be considered is: Did you reach the target audience? Tom Chant, Head of Customer Innovation at Telefónica UK, speaking at Big Brand Week in 2015, says this: "Regardless of any big numbers, if your campaign failed to connect with your target audience then there are definitely going to be some changes you need to make next time around."[3] At this point, you should have already spent at least some time figuring out personas and audiences at which to aim content. You've likely geared individual content pieces towards specific segments. If your content received any kind of views or engagement, which audience was the one that actually responded? Was that the intended effect?

Some metrics are specific to the type of platform. What follows is a breakdown of some the most common measurements used for each.[4]

BLOGS AND WEBSITES

+ **Page views.** This tells you which and how many of your pages are being consumed. It can help you to identify content that is popular and that may be worth revisiting, either to update or to repurpose in other formats.
+ **Unique visitors.** This statistic gives you a more realistic idea of the actual size of your audience, and can tell you also how many are returning readers.
+ **Average time spent.** Are people quickly scanning your content, or sticking around to consume it more in-depth?
+ **Page depth.** Are visitors coming to read just one thing, or are they exploring deeper? If they're interested, they won't leave after consuming just one piece of content.
+ **Bounce rate.** If someone only visits one page of your site or blog during their session, that is counted as a bounce. The more times this happens, the higher the bounce rate. This is related to page depth; readers who like your content won't just leave.

SOCIAL MEDIA

+ **Likes and favorites.** Mentioned earlier, these represent some of the most passive forms of engagement, but still show that people responded somehow.
+ **Comments.** These are valuable for demonstrating reader interest, and allow for a two-way conversation about the content not available with other types of responses.

+ **Shares.** The gold standard of engagement. It proves the value of the content, since it was useful or interesting enough for readers to want to distribute it to others.
+ **Follower count.** Generally speaking, this is one of the least meaningful metrics; however, it can make a difference when you notice a specific increase or drop in the number. This measurement can act as a red flag for problems or successes. If people suddenly stop following the account, go back and look to see what content may have triggered the decrease. Or, a specific piece of content may have gained followers, in which case you may want to create more, similar content.

Common Goals and Associated Metrics

ENGAGEMENT
Comments
Likes
Shares
Tweets
+1s
Pins
Forwards
Clickthroughs

PATRON LOYALTY
% content consumed
Repeat website/
blog visitors
E-mail subscriptions
and opt-outs

BRAND AWARENESS
Website traffic
Page views
Video views
E-mail opens
Document views
Downloads

Based on information from *The Complete Guide to Influencer Marketing: Strategies, Templates & Tools*, Content Marketing Institute, 2015

E-MAIL

+ **E-mails opened.** Most professional e-mail distribution services will tell you how many people opened a particular e-mail, and when it was opened.

+ **Link clicks.** The same software or service that can show you how many e-mails were opened can also tell you which links in those e-mails were the most popular.

+ **Unsubscribes/opt-outs.** Knowing how many people stop wanting your library's e-mails, especially after a particular notice, is one of the best ways to know whether or not people find the content useful. People generally don't unsubscribe from those things that they find valuable.

+ **Forwards.** It's not currently possible to always get accurate counts of how many times a particular e-mail is forwarded, because not all people use the forward function embedded in mass e-mails; many use the forwarding inherent in their e-mail clients. However, this number can give you some idea about the shareability of content, especially when compared to other e-mails your library has sent.

BOTTOM LINE: Not all metrics will be applicable to your platforms or campaigns. However, all measurements can help you gain insight into which types of content do best for your library. Metrics allow for the fine-tuning of content to meet stated goals.

Clear as Mud?

Unfortunately, no metrics, no matter which you choose, will tell you exactly how to be more effective (that's what this book is for!). However, metrics do give you a clearer picture of the areas in which you can improve. You can't know if you're making any headway, without benchmarking where you started from and where you are now.

There are also no magic numbers that you should be striving for. Having X number of comments on Y number of posts will, on its own merits, get you nowhere. Save yourself a lot of headache, and understand that your library is its own biggest competitor. Its progress is best measured against itself.

For many of us, assessing and analyzing the numbers is possibly one of the parts of content marketing that is most arduous. I'll be the first to admit that it's something I struggle with, primarily because it's not as interesting (to me) as some of the other facets of the content marketing process. Also, let's be honest here: sometimes, no matter who you are, looking at the numbers can be discouraging. It's not always good news, and sometimes even your most enthusiastically created content is a dud.

However, content marketing, no matter what kind you do or measure, is a game for the long term. Individual posts or content pieces fail or succeed, but it's only the long-haul results that really matter. Looking at the short term helps refine immediate work, but ongoing tracking enables your content marketing to evolve. The Columbus (OH) Metropolitan Library's Digital Strategy document, appended to the end of this chapter, is a good example of using metrics for ongoing assessment and adjustments to strategy.

BOTTOM LINE: Metrics are not always easy, but essential to your library's ongoing content marketing work. Don't just look at them every so often; keep a firm handle on what's happening to make your efforts count.

NOTES

1. Kevin Shively, "60% of Social Marketers Say Measuring ROI Is a Top Challenge in TrustRadius Survey," June 2, 2015, http://simplymeasured.com/blog/60-of -marketers-say-measuring-roi-is-top-challenge-in-trustradius-survey/ #i.1x2pyglygdep2v.
2. Leah Betancourt, "What Makes Content Marketing ROI Work," August 7, 2014, http://engage.scribblelive.com/Article/711280-What-Makes-Content -Marketing-ROI-Work.
3. Andy Vale, "How Do You Know If Your Social Media Plan Has Succeeded Or Failed?," April 22, 2015, www.socialbro.com/how-do-you-know-if -your-social-media-plan-succeeded-or-failed/.
4. Douglas Karr, "What Metrics to Measure Content Marketing Effectiveness With," April 23, 2015, https://www.marketingtechblog.com/content-marketing-metrics/.

Columbus Metropolitan Library
Digital Strategy Sample

COLUMBUS
METROPOLITAN
LIBRARY

columbuslibrary.org | 645-2275

Contact: Debra Pack, Marketing Manager, Columbus Metropolitan Library
614-849-1054, dpack@columbuslibrary.org

Columbus Metropolitan Library's Digital Strategy

Columbus Metropolitan Library (CML) is an organization driven by a Strategic Plan with three key strategies: Young Minds, My Library and Life Skills. The investments and desired outcomes are defined by the needs in the communities the library serves. The library's work in its digital channels is driven by the same three strategies.

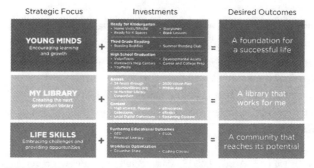

CML's Digital Strategy is a key investment in the My Library strategy to create the next generation library that works for its customers.

The Marketing Department is responsible for CML's Digital Strategy, in collaboration with the organization's Information Technology Department.

The tactics, goals and desired outcomes of the Digital Strategy are directly connected to the breadth of work of the organization.

WHAT WE DO

CML uses multiple digital channels to tell the library's story and drive its strategies. Data is a critical factor in determining how we allocate resources to our digital efforts. Google analytics, website heat maps and other email and social media tracking tools guide our work to reach multiple audiences. We partner with a local digital agency, Fathom, to ensure customers (and potential customers) find columbuslibrary.org when they search for key services and programs the library provides. This work in SEO (search engine optimization) is fundamental to CML's success it its digital strategy.

Digital strategy document from Columbus Metropolitan Library in Ohio.
Used with permission.

COLUMBUS
METROPOLITAN
LIBRARY

columbuslibrary.org | 645-2275

WHAT WE HAVE LEARNED

Online users change every year. Continued engagement requires diligence and understanding in order to meet our digital strategy goals. Analytics algorithms and the search engine optimization environment change rapidly; "under the hood" knowledge is critical to success. Investing in outsourcing this work provides high dividends; the critical "outside looking in" approach is of value for perspective and skill set.

HOW DATA IMPACTS WHAT WE DO
Data drives decisions on:
- Website design, content and how we write and tag it to increase SEO
- Website links and cross linking on authoritative sites
- Email strategy
- Social media strategy
- Incorporating external experiences (public catalog interface, app, eContent, streaming content) into the columbuslibrary.org experience

Some examples:

WEBSITE
Mobile Responsiveness:
In 2014, 28% of visits to CML's website were from mobile devices, and we are trending to 40% by the end of 2015. According to experts in the digital arena, mobile accounts for 60% of time spent using digital media overall.

Customers will leave a site that is not responsive. With the upgrade to Drupal 7 (website platform) in 2015, CML's website is now fully responsive. We're tracking in Google Analytics to see if mobile adoption rates rise with responsiveness. Because we've been intentionally tracking website visits in Google Analytics with the launch of a new website in 2012, we have benchmarks established.

We'll also launch a new public catalog experience and mobile app in the first quarter of 2016. We're curious to see how this impacts mobile visits as well.

Our services pages:
In 2014 we launched Reading Buddies, a service to help students K-3 increase their reading skills. This was in response to the state of Ohio's Third Grade Reading Guarantee, requiring all third graders to be proficient readers before advancing to fourth grade.

Early proficiency testing in schools showed there was much work to be done, so we launched a Third Grade Reading web page to provide our customers a place to go for information about the state's mandate, resources from the library and other organizations, and a schedule of times after school that students could come for one-on-one reading practice with staff and volunteers.

We had more than 13,000 page views on the Third Grade Reading page. But we felt those numbers could be higher with a more focused approach, so we are trying new tactics in 2015. We have split the information into two web pages:

- Third Grade Reading web page focused on information about the guarantee and resources for educators (Educator Tool Kit)

Digital strategy document from Columbus Metropolitan Library in Ohio.
Used with permission.

- Reading Buddies web page focused on the service, with tips for parents (Parent Tool Kit) to help their children practice reading

We're tracking visits and engagement on those pages to assess their success in 2016.

INTERACTIVE DIGITAL PRESENCE
Digital Downloads (eBooks, audiobooks, streaming content)

In 2014 we strived to increase online digital products downloads to 1 million.

Analytics showed we were trending slow to reach the goal so we increased cross promotion in all channels, including using printed pieces promoting Hoopla and Zinio in all locations.

We ultimately surpassed the goal by 0.2 million (for a total of 1.2 million).

In 2014, our eBooks website page had 416,554 page views with only 25% of users clicking through to OverDrive. This told us that we needed to refresh the way we drive customers to our Digital Downloads page on OverDrive. While we used a large image with "We have eBooks" prominently displayed on our homepage and other internal web pages, customers still told us they didn't know we had eBooks.

So in 2015, we revised our homepage to call out each digital channel in a cohesive way:

- eBooks and Audiobooks
- Music and Movies
- Magazines
- My History (our digital collections of photos, documents and artifacts)

We're tracking in Google Analytics and with heat maps to assess the success of this new tactic.

We also increased promotion in our emails and social media platforms to raise awareness and participated in OverDrive's key promotions like Big Library Reads.

Customer and Stakeholder Emails

This channel remains one of our most critical to drive traffic to our website and tell the library story to customers and stakeholders. We are able to easily highlight stories that further the work in our Young Minds, My Library and Life Skills strategies. We send bi-monthly Check It Out emails to all cardholders who provide an email address and monthly emails to stakeholders from CML's CEO.

In 2014 we increased our overall average open rate to 30% (24% in 2013), a better than average rate for nonprofits (26% according to various industry sources).

We increased our click-through rate to columbuslibrary.org 100% over 2013, through intentional linking in other channels, driving customers to our website where we are focused on content that furthers our organizational strategies.

Digital strategy document from Columbus Metropolitan Library in Ohio.
Used with permission.

COLUMBUS
METROPOLITAN
LIBRARY

columbuslibrary.org | 645-2275

The increase in open and click-through rates tells us our customers are interested in receiving emails from us. We will continue to use our resources to better understand how to reach our customers with increasing effectiveness.

In 2016 we plan to do A/B testing to try new content strategies. The results will drive refinements to our already successful email strategy.

Opt-in, Value-Add Emails:
We offer three emails to customers who want to sign up to receive this content:
1. *Ready for Kindergarten* focuses on early literacy skill building and kindergarten readiness
2. *Kindergarten and Beyond* focuses on school-age, primarily K-5, but offers content for teens who use our Homework Help Centers
3. *Local History and Genealogy* focuses on promoting resources and programs the library provides, including our My History digital collection of photos, documents and artifacts from the Columbus and central Ohio area.

In 2014 we had a goal to increase sign-ups of our opt-in emails by 10%. We reached this goal through intentional and consistent cross promotion in our channels.

Ready for Kindergarten and *Kindergarten and Beyond* opt-in emails averaged a 37% open rate and 8% click-through rate. Industry average for emails sent by nonprofits is a 26% open rate with 3% click-through rate.

The high open and click-through rates that continue after initial sign-up tells us this content is of value for our customers and is content we need to consistently repurpose in other channels. CML uses a content marketing strategy so this work falls into this strategy as well.

To increase opt-in email sign-ups in 2015, we're maximizing the benefits of traffic to our web pages by using prime real estate on our homepage to promote these emails, driving customers to the sign-up page on our website.

Social Media
We have 36,000+ followers on Facebook who have awareness of our brand. Facebook algorithms change frequently which impacts how well our posts perform. But one thing is clear: Facebook prefers posts that have very little focus on the organization but follow what is trending overall in social media across industries ⸱ lists, graphics and quotes. We have shifted our tactics as Facebook has shifted its business practices.

Improved Facebook Insights have been helpful in guiding when we need to pay to play for a critical organizational story needs to be shared. We can budget accordingly, so data is helping us determine our digital advertising budget.

Twitter is a key platform for us – 19,000 followers engage daily with us. We recently used Periscope to live stream a few events and we'll be assessing its viability.

We are gaining ground with Instagram and looking at new tactics to increase our reach.

Digital strategy document from Columbus Metropolitan Library in Ohio.
Used with permission.

Again, data tells us if a social media platform is effective in reaching our audiences but measuring true customer engagement is still a challenge, one that many brands are facing. We allocate resources to this goal, and seek out other marketers in varied industries to discuss.

ROI ON OUR DIGITAL STRATEGY AND ANALYTICS

As with any strategic focus, measurable outcomes are important. So we track visits, open rates, click-throughs, inbound traffic, outbound traffic, links on authoritative sites – so many digital touchpoints to consider.

Can we say for certain a customer checked out an individual book because it was featured on our website? Not without an inordinate amount of work and resources that wouldn't provide a strong return. But with analytics, can we see upward trends in check-out of the title when it is featured with a click-through to the catalog? Yes, we can. And that's of value to us for our circulation and collection strategies.

Can we say for certain that a customer receiving a Ready for Kindergarten email used the tips found in the email? Not without an inordinate amount of work and resources that wouldn't provide a strong return. But with analytics, can we be confident that this valuable content is reaching the customers who open our email? Yes, we can. And that's of value to us when we make decisions on types of content we focus our resources on to create.

In 2015 we turned our focus to measuring engagement more effectively, but what is the best way to do that? What are good numbers? Those are questions many brands, even big, for-profit ones, are struggling to determine.

But we all know this:
- Digital channels are critical to any organization's brand success
- SEO is key – it's very easy to drop off Google's radar if you aren't under the hood with their bots and algorithms
- Good content makes or breaks an organization's brand in digital spaces
- Brand awareness is valuable, whether it is measured in data or public good will

A strong digital strategy combined with a focused content strategy that employs analytics is critical to any organization's success in today's highly digital world.

Digital strategy document from Columbus Metropolitan Library in Ohio.
Used with permission.

Afterword

"Ain't nobody got time for that."
—Kimberly "Sweet Brown" Wilkins

If you've made it all the way through this book, then you already know you've probably got your work cut out for you. If you're starting your content marketing strategy from scratch, your process may look something like this:

1. **Panic.** This is harder than what we've been doing!
2. **Deep breath.** We can do this. We have to, to get our story out.
3. **Research.** Why are we telling our story?
4. **Personas.** To whom are we telling our story?
5. **Editorial calendar.** When are we telling our story, and where are we telling it?
6. **Content creation.** We're writing the chapters of our story.
7. **Measuring and evaluating.** Did people like our story?
8. **Go back and do steps 5–8 again.**

Perhaps the major takeaway from this book is that you need a process. It's no longer good enough to create content, willy-nilly, and distribute it when we have some extra time. We are now in an era where the sheer volume of available content is beyond what anyone can manage, and even getting eyeballs on our stuff is an uphill battle.

Afterword

We need to move library content marketing forward, understanding that this won't be a fast endeavor. We have to gear our content more for "youtility" than for promotion, and that won't be a simple mental shift for many of us to make. Our work needs to become data driven. It's time to ditch the anecdotal approach and start focusing on facts. We no longer have the luxury of only doing what we want, when we feel like it.

As content strategist Scott Abel says: "Content: there is no easy button."

Bibliography

Baer, Jay. Youtility: why smart marketing is about help not hype. New York: Portfolio/Penguin, 2013.

Betancourt, Leah. "What Makes Content Marketing ROI Work." Engage Magazine. August 7, 2014. http://engage.scribblelive.com/Article/711280-What-Makes -Content-Marketing-ROI-Work.

Bird, Chris. "5 reasons why your content marketing fails (and how to prevent it)." The Business Journals. August 20, 2015. www.bizjournals.com/bizjournals/how-to/ marketing/2015/08/5-reasons-why-content-marketing-fails.html?page=all.

Brennan, Matt. "Why Writing For The Web Is Important." Business 2 Community. April 16, 2015. www.business2community.com/communications/ writing-web-important-01207379.

Brogan, Chris. "How Do I Get People to Care About What I'm Doing?—Tell Bigger Stories." September 24, 2012. http://chrisbrogan.com/theflag.

Camplejohn, Doug. "Three Ways It Pays for Marketers to Be More Data-Driven." MarketingProfs. August 28, 2015. www.marketingprofs.com/articles/2015/28352three -ways-it-pays-for-marketers-to-be-more-data-driven.

Casel, Brain. "Writing and Designing a Killer Headline." Envanto Tuts+. 2013, http:// webdesign.tutsplus.com/articles/writing-and-designing-a-killer-headline --webdesign-16744.

Chapman, C.C. "Introduction to Content Marketing" Lynda.com. Oct 22, 2013. www .lynda.com/Content-Marketing-tutorials/Introduction-Content-Marketing/135355 -2.html?srchtrk=index:1%0Alinktypeid:2%0Aq:Introduction%2Bto%2BContent% 2BMarketing%0Apage:1%0As:relevance%0Asa:true%0Aproducttypeid:2.

Cohen, Heidi. "How to Craft Headlines That Draw People to Your Content." Social Media Examiner. March 18, 2015. www.socialmediaexaminer.com/how-to-craft -headlines-that-draw-people-to-your-content/.

Content Marketing Institute. "Content Marketing Framework: Plan." http://contentmarketinginstitute.com/plan/.

Bibliography

—— "2015 Nonprofit Content Marketing: Content Marketing Benchmarks, Budgets, and Trends—North America."http://contentmarketinginstitute.com/wp-content/uploads/2014/11/2015_NonProf_Research.pdf.

—— "What Is Content Marketing?: Useful content should be at the core of your marketing." http://contentmarketinginstitute.com/what-is-content-marketing/.

Copyblogger, "Content Marketing How to Build an Audience that Builds Your Business." www.copyblogger.com/content-marketing/.

Davis, Melanie. "How to Speak Like a Human (and Why It Matters)." *Convince & Convert.* www.convinceandconvert.com/content-marketing/how-to-speak-like-a-human-and-why-it-matters/.

Deckers, Eric. "Your Headlines Suck. Here's What You Can Do About It." *Convince & Convert.* www.convinceandconvert.com/content-marketing/your-headlines-suck-heres-what-you-can-do-about-it/.

Delzio, Suzanne. "Research Shows Metrics Marketers Think Matter Most." *Social Media Examiner.* January 13, 2015. www.socialmediaexaminer.com/research-shows-metrics-marketers-think-matter/.

—— "Social Sharing Habits: New Research Reveals What People Like to Share." *Social Media Examiner.* March 24, 2015. www.socialmediaexaminer.com/social-sharing-habits-new-research/.

D'Souza, Sean. "The Flashing Christmas Light Technique for Writing Irresistible Bullet Points." *Copyblogger.* www.copyblogger.com/irresistible-bullet-points/.

Ellering, Nathan. "10 Reasons Your Editorial Calendar Sucks (and How to Make It the Best)." *Convince & Convert.* www.convinceandconvert.com/content-marketing/improve-editorial-calendar/.

—— "How To Quadruple Your Traffic With A Social Media Editorial Calendar." *CoSchedule.* 2015. http://coschedule.com/blog/how-to-quadruple-your-traffic-with-a-social-media-editorial-calendar/.

Entrepreneur. "Why Influencer Marketing Pays Off for Small Businesses." February 27, 2015. http://finance.yahoo.com/news/why-influencer-marketing-pays-off-230000605.html;_ylt=A0LEVjgQVPNUH3IAmSslnIlQ.

Gaenzle, Anthony. "Why You Need to Conduct a Full Audit for Successful Content Marketing." *Content Marketing Institute.* March 14, 2014. http://contentmarketinginstitute.com/2014/03/conduct-full-audit-successful-content-marketing/.

Ganguly, Ishita. "7 Ways to Improve Your Social Media Engagement." *Social Media Examiner.* May 11, 2015. www.socialmediaexaminer.com/7-ways-to-improve-social-media-engagement/.

Bibliography

Gebauer, Susanna. "Repurposing Content or Cross-Posting—Efficiency vs. Spam." *The Social Ms.* December 1, 2014. http://blog.thesocialms.com/repurposing -content-cross-posting-efficiency-vs-spam/#XHTW000cZEu516yD.99.

Gioglio, Jessica. "3 Tactics to Surprise and Delight Your Fans." *Convince & Convert.* www .convinceandconvert.com/social-media-case-studies/surprise-and-delight/.

Glickman, Daniel. "How to Give Your Content Marketing Strategy a Complete Make-over." *Convince & Convert.* www.convinceandconvert.com/content-marketing/ update-your-content-marketing-strategy/.

Gray, Justin. "How to Drill Down to Your True Target Audience." *Convince & Convert.* www.convinceandconvert.com/social-media-strategy/ how-to-drill-down-to-your-true-target-audience/.

Handley, Ann. *Everybody Writes.* Hoboken, NJ: John Wiley & Sons, 2014.

Hanley, Ryan. "7 Ways to Fail at Content Marketing." November 4, 2014. www .ryanhanley.com/7-ways-to-fail-at-content-marketing/.

Harris, Jodi. "How to Measure the Success of Content Marketing." *Content Marketing Institute.* June 15, 2012. http://contentmarketinginstitute.com/2012/06/ measure-success-content-marketing/.

Hursh, Angela. "The Biggest Library Marketing Obstacles and How to Overcome Them." February 2, 2015. https://librarycontentmarketing.wordpress .com/2015/02/11/the-five-biggest-library-marketing-obstacles-and-how-to -overcome-them-with-content-marketing/.

Karr, Douglas. "Add These 2 Elements to Every Post, and Your Blog Will Explode in Popularity." *Marketing Tech Blog.* January 2, 2014. https://www.marketingtechblog .com/2-keys-to-success/.

——"What Makes a Good Headline?: Why Only 20% of Your Readers Are Clicking Through on Your Article Title." *Marketing Tech Blog.* August 19, 2014. https://www .marketingtechblog.com/write-incredible-titles-headlines/.

——"What Metrics to Measure Content Marketing Effectiveness With." *Marketing Tech Blog.* April 23, 2015. https://www.marketingtechblog.com/content-marketing-metrics/.

Kentico Marketing. "Quick Start Guide: Marketing Persona." https://www.kentico .com/Product/Resources/Quick-Start-Guides/Kentico-Marketing-Personas -Quick-Start-Guide/Marketing-Personas.

Kruse, Kathi. "10 Guaranteed Ways to #Fail at Content Marketing." *Kruse Control.* July 27, 2015. www.krusecontrolinc.com/ways-to-fail-at-content-marketing/.

Lee, Kevan. "The Complete Social Media Checklist for Writing Winning Posts." *Buffer.* April 6, 2015. https://blog.bufferapp.com/social-media-checklist.

Bibliography

——— "Marketing Personas: The Complete Beginner's Guide." March 27, 2014. https://blog.bufferapp.com/marketing-personas-beginners-guide.

——— "We Stopped Publishing New Blog Posts for One Month. Here's What Happened." *Buffer.* August 11, 2015. https://blog.bufferapp.com/blog-strategies.

Lee, Nancy R. and Philip T Kotler. *Marketing in the Public Sector: A Roadmap for Improved Performance.* Upper Saddle River, NJ: FT Press, 2006.

Lehr, Andrea. "New Research: How and When to Publish Content in Order to Score Big on Social Media." *Buffer.* April 7, 2015. https://blog.bufferapp.com/research-how-and-when-to-publish-content-social-media.

Lieb, Rebecca. "How to Conduct a Content Audit." *Marketing Land.* February 16, 2015. http://marketingland.com/conduct-content-audit-117781.

Lin, Aaron. "Write Like a Pro: 5 Techniques Top Bloggers Use to Write Successful Blog Posts." *Convince & Convert.* www.convinceandconvert.com/content-marketing/write-like-a-pro-5-techniques-top-bloggers-use-to-write-successful-blog-posts/.

Loranger, Hoa. "Break Grammar Rules on Websites for Clarity." *Nielsen Norman Group.* March 23, 2014. www.nngroup.com/articles/break-grammar-rules/.

McPhillips, Kathy. "A Simple Plan for Measuring the Marketing Effectiveness of Content." *Content Marketing Institute.* July 12, 2014. http://contentmarketinginstitute.com/2014/07/simple-plan-measuring-marketing-effectiveness-of-content/.

Marsh, Hilary. "How to Sell Content Strategy to Management." *UX Booth.* February 24, 2015. www.uxbooth.com/articles/how-to-sell-content-strategy-to-management/.

Mawhinney, Jesse. "17 Stats You Should Know About Visual Content Marketing in 2015." *HubSpot.* January 22, 2015. http://blog.hubspot.com/marketing/visual-content-marketing-strategy.

New York University. "Writing for the Web." https://www.nyu.edu/employees/resources-and-services/media-and-communications/styleguide/website/writing-for-the-web.html.

Norberg, Marti. "6 Ways To Fail At Content Marketing (Are You Guilty?)." *Zerys.* www.zerys.com/content-marketing-blog-1/bid/81560/6-Ways-To-Fail-At-Content-Marketing-Are-You-Guilty.

Ormond, Sally. This Is Why Content Marketing Is Important, *Briar Copywriting.* January 22, 2015. www.briarcopywriting.com/blog/this-is-why-content-marketing-is-important/.

Parker, Roger C. "A Checklist for Measuring Your Content Marketing Success." *Content Marketing Institute.* June 6, 2012. http://contentmarketinginstitute.com/2012/06/checklist-for-measuring-marketing-success/.

Bibliography

Polese, Leticia. "How Does Your Content Marketing Compare? [NEW DATA]." *SocialBro*. May 26, 2015. www.socialbro.com/blog/how-does-your-content-marketing -compare-new-data.

Quigg, Bridget. "5 Ways to Track Your Content on Social." *Simply Measured*. April 24, 2015. http://simplymeasured.com/blog/5-ways-to-track-your-content-on -social/#i.1x2pyglygdep2v.

——"10 Ways to Increase Your Engagement Overnight." *Simply Measured*. August 5, 2015. http://simplymeasured.com/blog/10-ways-to-increase-your-engagement -overnight-2/#i.1x2pyglygdep2v.

Nielsen, Jakob. "How Little Do Users Read?" *Nielsen Norman Group*. May 6, 2008. www .nngroup.com/articles/how-little-do-users-read/.

Patel, Neil. "The Formula for a Perfect Headline." *Quick Sprout*. July 3, 2014. www .quicksprout.com/2014/07/03/the-formula-for-a-perfect-headline/.

Polese, Leticia. "How Does Your Content Marketing Compare? [NEW DATA]." *SocialBro*. May 26, 2015. www.socialbro.com/how-does-your-content-marketing-compare -new-data/.

Radice, Rebekah. "Become a Content Marketing Powerhouse: Secrets to a Super-Sticky Strategy." May 18, 2015. http://rebekahradice.com/ become-a-content-marketing-powerhouse-secrets-to-a-super-sticky-strategy/.

—— "How to Create Visual Content Your Audience Will Love." August 3, 2015. http://rebekahradice.comcreate-visual-content-your-audience -will-love/.

Relevance. "Quick Guide for Content Marketing Research: The 4 Essential Research Assessments." http://digital.relevance.com/hubfs/Quick_Guide_for_Content _Marketing_Research.pdf.

Schaefer, Mark W. "10 Simple ideas to achieve more content sharing now." 2015. www.businessesgrow.com/2015/06/15/content-sharing/.

—— *The Content Code*. Mark W. Schaefer, 2015.

Sobal, Alex. "The Difference Between Content Promotion and Content Distribution." *Whole Brain Marketing Blog*. December 22, 2014. www.weidert.com/whole_brain _marketing_blog/the-difference-between-content-promotion-and-content -distribution.

Shively, Kevin. "60% of Social Marketers Say Measuring ROI Is a Top Challenge in TrustRadius Survey." *Simply Measured*. June 2, 2015. http://simplymeasured.com/ blog/60-of-marketers-say-measuring-roi-is-top-challenge-in-trustradius-survey/ #i.1x2pyglygdep2v.

Bibliography

Shorr, Brad. "Five Copywriting Errors That Can Ruin A Company's Website." *Smashing Magazine*. June 29, 2011. www.smashingmagazine.com/2011/06/five-copywriting -errors-that-can-ruin-a-company-website/.

Sierra, Jeff. "These Mistakes Can Make Your Content Marketing an Epic Failure (but You Can Avoid Them)." *MarketingProfs*. June 25, 2015. www.marketingprofs.com/ articles/2015/27929/these-mistakes-can-make-your-content-marketing-an-epic -failure-but-you-can-avoid-them.

Single Grain. "The Step-by-Step Guide to Conducting a Content Audit." http:// singlegrain.com/the-step-by-step-guide-to-conducting-a-content-audit/.

Slater, Jeffrey. "Change the Channel to Ignite Content." 2015. www.businessesgrow .com/2015/04/23/ignite-content/.

Stelzner, Michael. "Google Analytics: How to Know If Your Marketing is Working." *Social Media Examiner*. February 20, 2015. www.socialmediaexaminer.com/ google-analytics-with-christopher-penn/.

Usability.gov. "Writing for the Web." www.usability.gov/how-to-and-tools/methods/ writing-for-the-web.html.

Vale, Andy. "How Do You Know If Your Social Media Plan Has Succeeded Or Failed?" *SocialBro*. April 22, 2015. www.socialbro.com/how-do-you-know-if-your-social -media-plan-succeeded-or-failed/.

Watercutter, Angela. "How Oreo Won the Marketing Super Bowl with a Timely Blackout Ad on Twitter." *Wired*. February 4, 2013. www.wired.com/2013/02/ oreo-twitter-super-bowl/.

Webster, Tom. "How to Use Research to Create Content That Works." *Convince & Convert*. www.convinceandconvert.com/podcasts/episodes/ use-research-to-create-content-that-works/.

Wittlake, Eric. "If you can't measure marketing ROI, find the right alternative." 2015. www.businessesgrow.com/2015/07/22/marketing-roi/.

Wordstream.com. "The Expert's Guide to Keyword Research for Social Media." www .wordstream.com/articles/keyword-research-for-social-media-guide.

Index

Index

Index

Index

Index

Index

Sobal, Alex, 19–20
social media
    Anthony Juliano on content
        marketing, 13–16
    channels in editorial calendar, 48–49
    ego in, 2
    engagement with posts, 85–86
    library mistakes in promotion via, 12
    measurement of content marketing,
        questions for, 90
    metrics for measurement of content
        marketing, 91–94
    re-purposed content, 52–54
    sample social sharing calendar,
        50–51
    user-generated content analysis, 30
    visual content for, 83–84
    Youtility concept and, 4
social sharing calendar
    example of, 50–51
    guidance for, 48–49
Socialbakers.com, 71
spreadsheet
    for content audit, 44–45
    for editorial calendar, 47
staff
    cost of content marketing, 76
    experience, ignoring, 76–77
    as source of content, 55
staff favorites, 15
stories
    of library staff, 77
    mistake of not using stories from real
        people, 81
    of mistakes by library staff, 85–86
    in online content, 69
strategy
    characteristics of effective content
        marketing, 17

    effective content marketing as
        strategic, 18
    writing strategy guide, 57–60
subheadings, 72
subsections, 72
success
    definition of in content strategy, 60
    metrics for measurement of content
        marketing, 96
survey, 30–31

T

target audience
    measurement of reaching, 92
    mistake of using "one size fits all"
        plan, 82
targeting
    characteristics of effective content
        marketing, 17
    content marketing *vs.* content
        promotion, 19–21
    content strategy for, 59
    focus on particular audience, 18
text, 84
themes, 48
time, 93
    See also editorial calendar
tone, of online content, 68
topic, matching to content type, 48
tragedy, library provision of resources
        for, 56
trust
    content marketing for, 24
    online advertising and, 23
TrustRadius, 89
tutorials, 55
tweets
    engagement metric, 91–92
    promotion *vs.* marketing, 20